1995

Sustainable Democracy is a joint report of twenty-one social scientists, from ten countries and four academic disciplines, who collaborated over the period of two years under the name of the Group on East–South Systems Transformations (ESST). Their report identifies the principal political and economic choices confronting new democracies in southern and Eastern Europe and South America, while evaluating their merits and feasibility in the light of current social science knowledge.

The authors explore the social, political, and economic conditions under which democracy is likely to generate desirable and politically desired objectives, as well as whether it is likely to last. They argue that the state has an essential role in promoting universal citizenship and in creating conditions for sustained economic growth. Special emphasis is placed on the interdependence between political and economic reforms.

SUSTAINABLE DEMOCRACY

Adam Przeworski

Pranab Bardhan, Luiz Carlos Bresser Pereira, László Bruszt,
Jang Jip Choi, Ellen Turkish Comisso, Zhiyuan Cui,
Torcuato di Tella, Elemer Hankiss, Lena Kolarska-Bobińska,
David Laitin, José María Maravall, Andranik Migranyan,
Guillermo O'Donnell, Ergun Ozbudun, John E. Roemer,
Philippe C. Schmitter, Barbara Stallings, Alfred Stepan,
Francisco Weffort, Jerzy J. Wiatr

SUSTAINABLE DEMOCRACY

CAMBRIDGE
UNIVERSITY PRESS

Published by the Press Syndicate of the University of Cambridge
The Pitt Building, Trumpington Street, Cambridge CB2 1RP
40 West 20th Street, New York, NY 10011–4211, USA
10 Stamford Road, Oakleigh, Melbourne 3166, Australia

First published 1995

Printed in the United States of America

Library of Congress Cataloging-in-Publication Data
Sustainable democracy / Adam Przeworski with Pranab Bardhan . . . [et al.].
p.   cm.
A joint report by 21 authors, working together as the Group on
East–South Systems Transformations; A. Przeworski wrote some of the
text and edited all of the papers.
Includes bibliographical references.
ISBN 0–521–48261–5. – ISBN 0–521–48375–1 (pbk.)
1. Democracy – Case studies. 2. Economic development – Case
studies. 3. Post-communism – Case studies. I. Przeworski, Adam.
II. Group on East–South Systems Transformations.
JC423.S94   1995
321.8'094 – dc20   94–47142
                                                            CIP

A catalog record for this book is available from the British Library.

ISBN 0–521–48261–5 hardback
ISBN 0–521–48375–1 paperback

Contents

Preface

The purpose of *Sustainable Democracy* is to sketch a map of politically pressing and intellectually challenging issues facing new democracies in the South and the East. We seek to identify the principal political and economic choices confronting new democracies and to evaluate the merits and the feasibility of the alternatives in the light of current social science knowledge.

Our concerns originate from two observations, which are by now trivial. The past decade witnessed an unprecedented, worldwide movement toward political democracy simultaneously with a profound, also widespread, economic stagnation. In the past fifteen years, many countries in southern Europe, Latin America, Asia, and Africa have held competitive elections, the first ever or at least the first in decades. And since this project was initiated, this list has extended to Eastern Europe and several new countries that have emerged from the breakdown of the Soviet Union and Yugoslavia.[1] Never have so many countries enjoyed or at least experimented with democratic institutions. At the same time, models of economic development, which were quite successful during several decades, seem to have collapsed in many countries. The economic crises in the 1980s facing Argentina, Brazil, and Mexico as well as Bulgaria, Hungary, and Poland are without precedent in the history of these nations. As a result, we seem to witness simultaneously an almost fatalistic recognition of economic constraints and a frantic search for new models and new strategies to generate sustained growth. The standard prescriptions emanating from Washington and the international financial institutions are socially costly and economically dubious, yet the situation seems so tightly constrained by the gravity of the crisis and by international pressures that it appears to leave no alternatives.

These notes are intended to offer a catalog of issues that emerge in those countries that are undergoing simultaneously processes of democratic change and economic transformation. Our purpose is to identify the choices that confront political forces in countries with vastly different histories, to look at a distance, trying to overcome both the fragmentation inherent in scholarly pursuits and the preoccupation with the current moment that obsesses scholars who not only study but also live daily through major transformations. We seek to summarize what we do know and to specify what we, as social scientists, do not know.

Our purpose is to identify and evaluate alternatives. The fall of communism in Eastern Europe has been widely interpreted as a triumph of democracy and of capitalism, and it is. Yet both democratic institutions and capitalist economies differ in significant ways even among the developed democratic countries. Moreover, those who seek to imitate these countries often forget that there are many cases in which capitalism has failed in generating either prosperity or democracy. While important political forces in many parts of the world grope for a way toward the "First World" – the "West" for some, the "North" for others – they confront choices in designing their political and economic institutions and in selecting the paths that would lead to freedom and prosperity. And these choices have consequences.

We are living in a highly ideological epoch. Several countries, particularly but not only in Eastern Europe, have or are about to venture into the greatest experiment since the forced Stalinist industrialization of 1929. The economic transformations envisaged in these countries ironically mirror the socialist project. They implement an intellectual blueprint, a blueprint developed within the walls of the North American academia and shaped by international financial institutions. They are radical: they are intended to turn upside down all the existing social relations. And they offer a single panacea, a magic wand, which, once waved, will cure all the ills. For the first time in history, capitalism is being adopted as an application of a doctrine, rather than evolving as a historical process of trial and error.

The neoliberal ideology emanating from the United States and the multinational agencies claims that the course to follow is obvious. This ideology is based on a belief about the virtues of markets and private ownership that is not justifiable in the light of contemporary economic theory, including neoclassical theory. It values efficiency over distribution to the extent of justifying social horrors. It places economic considerations over political ones, willing to sacrifice other economic and political values at the altar of efficiency. It is based on a profound conviction that there is only one way and that this way must be followed: not only any opposition but even discussion is portrayed as self-interested, "populist" reaction.[2] Proponents of this ideology argue as if they possessed a Last Judgment archetype of the world: a general model of economic and political dynamics that allows one to evaluate the ultimate consequences of all the partial steps.

Yet this model is but a conjecture, based on a mixture of evidence, argument from first principles, self-interest and wishful thinking. Moreover, this is not even the model that developed capitalist countries follow in their own practice: Western advisors are in the duplicitous situation of having to say, as Stiglitz (1992: 162) put it, "Do as we say, not as we do."

We do not seek to offer alternative blueprints, only to emphasize that any quest for democracy and prosperity necessarily involves alternatives, choices, and decisions. Choices are inevitable. And, as long as masses of people experience material deprivation, any notion of the end of conflicts is illusory.

Since we are looking toward the future, our views also inevitably combine evidence, argument from first principles, and wishful thinking. But one way to control our own prejudices is to introduce some skepticism by asking what will happen if the various alternative solutions we analyze fail: fail to satisfy the expectations they raise, fail to bring about democracy, prosperity and international cooperation. We disagree among ourselves about several crucial points and thus, having listed arguments and evidence in favor of and against various alternatives, we leave a number of issues unresolved. These disagreements constitute prima facie evidence that the alternatives are real and the issues they raise are not simple.

This document is a joint product of twenty-one social scientists, from ten countries and four academic disciplines, who collaborated over the period of two years under the name of the Group on East–South Systems Transformations (ESST).

The initial idea of forming such a group was due to Guillermo O'Donnell who, as president of the International Political Science Association, invited Adam Przeworski and Jerzy J. Wiatr to convene social scientists from the "South" and the "East" in an effort to exchange experiences and reflections concerning the double transition to democracy in the political realm and to a reliance on markets in the economic realm.

The group met four times, prepared and discussed a number of working papers, and, having developed friendship and mutual confidence, collaborated in the preparation of *Sustainable Democracy*. Various parts of the book were drafted by particular members of the group. The introductory and concluding sections were initially written by Adam Przeworski. Various segments of Part I resulted from the collaboration of several members: Lena Kolarska-Bobińska, Ellen Turkish Comisso, José María Maravall, Guillermo O'Donnell, Ergun Ozbudun, Adam Przeworski, Philippe C. Schmitter, Barbara Stallings, Alfred Stepan, Torcuato Di Tella, and Jerzy J. Wiatr. Chapter 1 is due almost entirely to David Laitin. Chapter 2 is based on ideas contained in an unpublished paper by O'Donnell (1992). Chapter 3 was drafted in large part by José María Maravall and Torcuato di Tella. Chapter 4 is a revised version of a draft by Luiz Carlos Bresser Pereira, José María Maravall, and Adam Przeworski. The first half of Chapter 5 was drafted by Zhiyuan Cui and the second part by Pranab Bardhan and John Roemer. Subsequently, Adam Przeworski edited the entire text, relying on advice from Emily Loose, Alex Holzman, and two anonymous reviewers, as well as on comments by almost all participants.

The fact that this is a joint product does not imply that all members of the group can assume the responsibility for the entire book. Indeed, since the group was highly heterogeneous in terms of intellectual styles, cultural traditions, and political orientations, several disagreements are evident in the text, and several formulations reflect an uneasy compromise. Moreover, we all suffered from disciplinary limitations and had to place our trust in the specialized expertise of our colleagues.

The list of working papers that served as the background for the book is included; the papers are available from Adam Przeworski at the University of Chicago or directly from the authors. Several of these articles have been published in journals in the United States and abroad.

Acknowledgments

This work was supported by a grant from the John D. and Catherine T. MacArthur Foundation. We are not only grateful for the support, but in this era of bureaucratic ossification, we particularly appreciate that the foundation was willing to commit its funds to such a risky undertaking. The Rockefeller Foundation generously extended its hospitality at the Bellagio Conference Center.

All throughout, we enjoyed invariably competent administrative support and research assistance from José Antonio Cheibub. Camille Busette-Hsu served as the support staff at the Bellagio meeting. Mike Alvarez prepared a summary of the literature concerning the impact of political institutions, while several other graduate students in the Department of Political Science at the University of Chicago contributed ideas and bibliographic services. We should also like to thank several Turkish, Hungarian, and Spanish colleagues who welcomed us in their respective countries and shared their ideas about the project.

Introduction

The Background: Modernization via Internationalization

The postwar experiences of the communist East and of several countries in the capitalist South have constituted two distinct attempts to overcome underdevelopment and to establish economic and political independence. The Eastern European model has been one of state property of productive resources, allocation by centralized command, and an autarkic development strategy led by producer-goods industries. The Latin American pattern was based on private property, an active role for the state, and a fair dose of protectionism oriented toward import-substitution industrialization. Both the East and the South were dependent parts of larger international systems: major decisions about investment, production, and pricing were made beyond the borders of particular countries. The Eastern European system was dominated by a single center, and allocations were overtly political, while in the South it was possible to play off competing centers against each other, and decisions were made by less visible private institutions.

Both strategies were successful during a long period, and several countries established significant industrial bases. According to Summers, Kravis, and Heston (1984: Table 1), the average annual rates of growth of real GDP (gross domestic product) between 1950 and 1980 for countries starting at different levels in 1950 were 3.9 percent for the Third World countries that started at a low level, 5.8 percent for those Third World countries that started at middle levels, 5.4 percent for the planned economies, and 4.1 percent for the industrial economies. Market economies grew at the average rate of 4.4 percent per annum, planned economies at the rate of 5.4 percent. By another count, from 1960 to 1980, the GDP of Latin American countries grew at an unweighted average of 5.2 percent while in Eastern Europe the rate of growth of the NMP (net material product) exceeded 6.0 percent. Several countries, including Romania and Brazil, experienced periods when industrial production grew at a two-digit rate. Yet this development simply collapsed both in the capitalist South and in the communist East in the 1980s. According to the World Bank (1987: Table 2.6), per capita income of countries at the middle level of development fell between 1980 and 1986 at the average rate of 0.3 percent per year. Between 1980 and 1985, the average GDP growth rate in Latin America was zero percent. By another count (IMF 1992: 34), per capita income declined in Latin America at the rate of 0.4 percent between 1983 and 1991. During these years the three Eastern European countries that furnished data to the IMF – Hungary, Poland, and Yugoslavia – had an average growth rate of 1.0 percent. Per capita consumption fell in many countries, while inequality increased almost everywhere. Neither model succeeded in generating self-sustaining growth.

Five explanations of this collapse compete: (1) The rapid rates of growth were possible only as long as development was extensive, little constrained by the scarcity of material and labor inputs; (2) the economic models, with their respective roles for the state as the architect of development strategies, could work only when economies were relatively simple;[3] (3) the post-1975 international conjuncture – the sudden increase in the price of oil and some other primary inputs, combined with foreign debt and a turn toward fiscal austerity in the developed countries – undermined development strategies based on import-substitution industrialization; (4) development strategies – heavy-industry-oriented autarky in the East and consumer-durables-oriented protection in the South – could not lead to a self-sustained development because they generated a permanent foreign exchange crisis; (5) corruption and capital flight in the South, along with higher levels of unproductive, particularly military expenditures in the East, absorbed a growing proportion of the economic surplus. Yet thus far, no one has established a compelling empirical case that would favor any one of these explanations at the expense of rival hypotheses.

The mere fact that the collapse of growth occurred almost simultaneously in several countries of Latin America and Eastern Europe may indicate common underlying causes. The view according to which command economies arrived at an economic crisis because of their inherent inefficiency is, therefore, not obvious. Moreover, while it is apparent that command economies were inefficient, empirical evidence based on the neoclassical model fails to show any systematic differences between Eastern European and developed Western economies in terms of technical efficiency, foreign trade efficiency, allocative efficiency, and even dynamic efficiency (Murrell, 1991). Hence, while the relative inefficiency of Eastern European economies seems prima facie obvious, the reasons for it escape the neoclassical theory. Militarization of the communist economies and the global extension of the strategic concerns of the Soviet Union may provide an alternative explanation of their economic decline. But then the question of why Latin American economies experienced a crisis of a similar magnitude more or less at the same moment remains particularly puzzling.

Why did Eastern Europeans massively reject their economic system while Latin Americans did not? As one compares the relative economic performance of Poland and Argentina over the past ten years, one would not predict from any economic statistics that one system would collapse and the other would not. Yet whereas Brazilians tend to see their deprivation as the result of injustice, in Poland survey respondents attributed their misery to the irrationality of the communist system.[4] One obvious reason was the visible demonstration effect of Western Europe: a comparison that became increasingly humiliating as time went on. ''Why cannot East Germany be like West Germany?'': this is the question to which the answer eventually became ''the economic system.'' While people living under communism could see successful capitalist economies, once the crisis set in, people living under capitalism did not have any paradigms of success under command economies.

While the causes of the collapse of growth in the South and the East are not obvious, the response to it seems easier to identify. It is best described as ''modernization via internationalization.'' Different political forces in the capitalist South and the post-communist East see no alternative but to embark on the ''North-West Passage'': a road that would lead their societies to the First World, for some the North, for others the West. This is a strategy of adopting political, economic, and cultural organization already existing elsewhere:[5] democracy, markets, and an individualistic, consumption-oriented culture that dominates the advanced capitalist world. In this strategy, modernization becomes synonymous with internationalization: integration into the world economy, combined with an imitation of economic, political, and cultural patterns prevalent in the advanced capitalist countries.

The political and economic program that guides the most important political forces all over Eastern Europe is to join the West, by (re)entering Europe. This program is based on a particular mode of reasoning, which can be dubbed ''the Eastern European syllogism.'' The main premise of this syllogism is, ''If not for communism, we would have been like the West.'' The minor premise asserts, ''Now communism is gone.'' The conclusion not only asserts that Eastern Europe should and will now embrace the Western model, but also promises that this model will generate the glitter and glamour of developed capitalism. And similar tones can now be heard from Latin America, whether in Salinas de Gortari's and Carlos Menem's promises to take their countries to ''the First World'' or in Collor de Mello's program of *integracao competitiva* (competitive integration).[6]

This strategy constitutes a turning point. Most postwar attempts at modernization conceived of development as a project of national economic and political independence. They asserted the importance of national cultures, they called for political institutions consistent with national traditions, and they envisaged growth led by national industries and oriented toward local markets.[7] In contrast, the strategy of modernization by internationalization voluntarily accepts at least a partial surrender of national sovereignty in the political, economic, and cultural realms.[8] This strategy opens local markets to foreign penetration, it abolishes cultural barriers, and it models political institutions on patterns developed elsewhere. Coca-Cola is no longer the drug of imperialist domination but the nectar of universal prosperity.

This strategy combines imitation with international integration. Imitation in the political realm: while, since World War II, democracy was a value almost all regimes revindicated, this was democracy with adjectives that were supposed to reflect national traditions, local cultures, or ideological projects. In various conceptions, democracy had to be participatory, direct, "popular," or consensualist. It had to extend beyond the political realm: democracy had to be economic, industrial, social. Imitation in the cultural realm: the culture of advanced capitalism, as epitomized by the United States, was widely rejected as materialistic, "consumption-oriented," individualistic, selfish. Various theories claimed that this culture is but an artificial product of capitalism and sought alternatives.[9] Imitation in the economic realm: markets were rejected not only as unjust but as irrational, private ownership as exploitative. All these alternatives disappeared almost overnight. Today, modernization means liberal democracy, consumption-oriented culture, and capitalism.

Why do we find this dramatic change? While domestic political and economic considerations certainly play a role, the simultaneity of these changes in various parts of world suggests that international factors are decisive. The latter are of two distinct types. On the one hand, several trends combined to create the environment in which the less developed countries, including those in Latin America and Eastern Europe, had to operate. On the other hand, specific actions by international actors provide the pressure for change.

In terms of the environment, at least four clusters of factors took on new force during the 1980s. First, the globalization of production and finance created a context where the old style of national independence became increasingly hard to defend. The rise of the "transplant" industries and of global subcontracting makes it difficult to distinguish a U.S. car or computer from ones made in Europe or Japan, or even Mexico or South Korea. Fencing off countries via protection thus becomes onerous, and the cost is magnified by the rapid diffusion of new technologies that transform international competitiveness. Financial integration, in turn, makes independent exchange and interest rate policies difficult to pursue and facilitates capital flight. These transformations were dramatically demonstrated in the early 1980s by the experience of the French Socialist government, which was forced to abandon its expansionist policy under international pressure. A new political and ideological force superimposed itself on this global economic environment. Second, the emergence in rapid succession of Margaret Thatcher, Ronald Reagan and Helmut Kohl as leaders of three important industrial countries established neoliberalism as the central ideological force in the Western world. And this new force appeared to be reinforced by the third trend: the powerful role of the model of economic growth adopted in East Asia. Whether by design or accident, these countries were frequently portrayed as examples of laissez faire open economies. Other Third World countries were told that if they would only emulate the ''Asian Tigers,'' they too could achieve development. Finally, the end of the Cold War and the disintegration of the Soviet Union eliminated both an alternative development model, however flawed it was in practice, and a source of finance for those wanting to follow a different path.

As the international context was shifting, specific pressures were being exerted to bring about changes in economic policy. After Mexico's near default in 1982, the banks cut off finance to virtually all Latin American countries. In order to avoid default, which few governments saw as a viable option, bargains had to be struck with the International Monetary Fund and the World Bank. The conditionality that the international financial institutions required in exchange for their loans was initially the traditional demand-management package. By 1985, however, the ''Baker Plan'' had shifted the emphasis to structural reforms: especially trade liberalization and a reduced role for the state. Unlike the situation in the 1970s, in the 1980s there was a united front of creditors. An alliance of the international financial institutions, the private banks, and the Thatcher–Reagan–Kohl governments was willing to use its political and economic power to back its ideological predilections.

This combination of the general international environment and specific pressures narrowed the policy options for Third World governments in financial difficulty. Some governments enthusiastically adopted the neoliberal policy package, while others complied reluctantly for lack of alternatives (Stallings 1992a and 1992b).

Laurence Whitehead (1991) and Philippe Schmitter (1991) made a similar argument with regard to the external influence on the process of democratization. Whitehead identified three processes through which international actors bring pressure to bear for democratization: contagion, consent, and control; Schmitter added a fourth: conditionality. Contagion refers to the diffusion of experiences from one country to another, essentially by demonstration effect. This mechanism has led to "waves" of democratization, of which the most recent is still under way. Consent is also a voluntary mechanism, involving the promotion of norms by international groups, such as the nongovernmental organizations. Control and conditionality, in contrast, entail sanctions for governments that do not comply with policy prescriptions of, respectively, bilateral and multilateral donors. Political conditionality is a recent extension of the more familiar economic conditionality referred to earlier. Thus, governments of the industrial countries and the World Bank have joined forces to condition aid on the elimination of corruption, protection of human rights, limits on arms expenditures, and, in some cases, steps toward democracy. The European Union has specifically limited membership to democracies – an important constraint on East European countries hoping to join it – and even in the Western Hemisphere the long-moribund Organization of American States recently has made some attempts to defend democracy in Haiti and Peru.

The crucial question with regard to modernization via internationalization – orienting production and consumption according to the prices and practices of international markets – is whether it will work. It is sobering to observe how many strategies of modernization have failed in the past. As Table 1 shows, joining the club of democracy and prosperity is a rare feat. Since World War II, only Cyprus, Greece, Japan, Portugal, South Korea, and Spain entered the First World, while Mexico and Taiwan may be at the door.[10]

Moreover, at least two of the countries just mentioned did not follow the neoliberal policies advocated for the Third World today. Japan and South Korea followed a distinctive economic strategy: they protected their domestic markets and allowed little foreign capital to enter, while the only form of openness was the promotion of exports. At the same time, the state played a significant role in all three countries, as well as in Spain, through financial subsidies, export incentives, and industrial policies (Amsden 1989, Haggard 1990, Wade 1990, Westphal 1990).

Even in those cases where modernization was a strategy of autonomous national development, it tended to create enormous tensions, since it generated changes in the distribution of income, shifts in power relations, and profound cultural transformations. While one can find arguments in favor of and against the prospects of success, the most likely outcome of the strategy

Table 1. *The "First World": democracies that by 1988 had a per capita income of at least 5,000 1985 PPP USD*

Country	Level in 1951[a]	Regime in 1951	Level in 1988
Canada	6,972	DEM	16,272
United States	8,989	DEM	18,339
Uruguay[b]	4,471	DEM	5,163
Israel	2,583	DEM	9,412
Japan[c]	1,580	DEM	12,209
South Korea[c,d]	822	AUT	5,156
Austria	2,701	DEM	11,201
Belgium	4,250	DEM	11,495
Cyprus[c,d]	2,039	AUT	7,858
Denmark	4,320	DEM	12,089
Finland	3,462	DEM	12,360
France	3,884	DEM	12,190
Germany	3,377	DEM	12,604
Greece[b,c]	1,299	DEM	5,857
Iceland	4,148	DEM	13,204
Ireland	2,681	DEM	6,239
Italy	2,732	DEM	11,741
Luxembourg	5,578	DEM	13,933
Netherlands	3,969	DEM	11,468
Norway	4,277	DEM	14,976
Portugal[c,d]	1,146	AUT	5,321
Spain[c,d]	2,105	AUT	7,406
Sweden	5,008	DEM	12,991
Switzerland	7,121	DEM	16,155
United Kingdom	5,121	DEM	11,982
Australia	5,704	DEM	13,321
New Zealand	5,234	DEM	9,864

Note: PPP USD refers to purchasing power parity, U.S. dollars; DEM, democratic; AUT, authoritarian.
[a] 1953 in Israel, Japan, and South Korea; 1960 in Cyprus.
[b] Suffered an authoritarian interlude between 1951 and 1988.
[c] Per capita income below 2,500 1985 PPP USD when first observed.
[d] Authoritarian regime in 1951.

of internationalization is an increase of economic disparities and an accompanying rise of political and cultural tensions.

In some ways, modernization by internationalization mitigates these tensions. Groping toward the First World need not entail mindless imitation: it may lead to a successful adaptation to the new international context. The structure of choices is different for latecomers, and as the example of Japan

Table 2. *Long-term trends of per capita GDP growth by region (percentages)*

Region or group	1913–1950	1950–1989
Asia	−0.1	3.6
Latin America	1.2	1.2
Sub-Saharan Africa		0.8
Europe, Middle East, and North Africa		2.0
Eastern Europe	1.4	2.0
Developing economies		2.7
OECD members	1.1	2.3

Source: World Bank (1991: Table 1.1).

illustrates, imitating policies or institutions of the more developed countries may be a form of inventive adaptation, rather than one of passive acceptance. Indeed, latecomers may be advantaged in the economic realm by increased opportunities for export earnings and export-related employment (Krueger 1991)[11] and in the political realm by the external pressures toward adopting and maintaining democratic institutions, discussed earlier. Any analysis of the current prospects must incorporate these temporal and spatial shifts in parameters.

Integration in the international markets opens opportunities for export-oriented production, and when accompanied by an opening of the internal markets, it leads to a more efficient allocation of resources. Although the causal direction is unclear, the statistical evidence is overwhelming that trade is positively related to growth.[12] Moreover, in spite of all the controversies about advantages and disadvantages of latecomers, statistical evidence shows again that, over the long run, rates of growth increased on a worldwide scale until the 1980s. The early European growth rates were 0.74 between 1800 and 1850, 1.27 between 1850 and 1900, and 1.35 between 1900 and 1950, while according to Maddison (1982) the growth rate of "industrial economies" between 1950 and 1980 was 3.1, and of the world as a whole it was 2.7. The long-term trends of per capita GDP growth by region are shown in Table 2 (World Bank 1991: Table 1.1). While output per person doubled in fifty-eight years in the United Kingdom from 1780, it doubled in forty-seven years in the United States from 1839, in thirty-four years in Japan from 1885, in twenty years in Turkey from 1857, in eighteen years in Brazil from 1961, in eleven years in South Korea from 1966, and in just ten years in China from 1977 (World Bank 1991: 12). Thus, developing later may mean growing faster.

Moreover, internationalization can take the form of integration in regional markets and political institutions. The countries of southern and, more recently, those of Eastern Europe have opted for associating with a concrete set of common institutions and obligations, namely, the European Union. These institutions offer not only an access to markets, but also rather significant subsidies and transfers for the benefit of the less developed members. Moreover, the European Union established early its political credibility, by insisting that all its members be stable, functioning democracies (without defining narrowly what this entailed). Entry into the European Union was of major importance for the consolidation of both economic policy and democratic institutions in Greece, Portugal, and Spain. It remains to be seen whether the Union will respond in as generous a fashion to the applications of the Czech Republic, Slovakia, Hungary, and Poland, not to mention Bulgaria, Romania, or the Baltic republics.

A similar option for regionalism as the preferred means for entering the First World can be observed in Latin America, in the efforts of Mexico and, eventually, Chile to enter into a free trade area with the United States and Canada, or in those of Brazil, Argentina, Uruguay, and Paraguay to form a South American common market of their own. These strategies, however, are much less appealing than in the case of Europe, given both the absence of strong international institutions to adjudicate disputes as well as redistribute benefits, and the overwhelming regional hegemony of a single actor, the United States.

While expanded economic opportunities, pressures toward democracy, and possibilities of regional integration speak in favor of the strategy of internationalization, other considerations forecast major difficulties. Internationalization is, by definition, a competitive strategy: while some regions, sectors, firms, or social groups may develop comparative advantage within the emerging international system, this strategy will inevitably generate winners and losers. Every country cannot be a net exporter. Moreover, the winners and the losers will not be nation-states but regions, sectors, industries, firms, or particular social groups. Hence, this strategy will generate, and already has produced, a sharp increase of regional, sectoral, and social inequality across and within nations.[13] Longer trends in inequality show that while Asian countries caught up since 1973 with the income of the OECD countries, the ratio of per capita GDP of Latin American, Eastern European, and sub-Saharan countries to that of the OECD countries declined between 1973 and 1989 (Table 3).

At the same time, the strategy of internationalization requires national

Table 3. *Ratio of per capita GDP to that of OECD countries*

Region or group	1830	1913	1950	1973	1989
Asia	40	23	15	16	28
Latin America		49	52	40	31
Sub-Saharan Africa			11	8	5
Eastern Europe	64	57	65	63	56
Developing economies		32	25	22	28

Source: World Bank (1991: Table 1.1).

governments to alienate some traditional instruments of economic policy: they peg exchange rates and adjust demand to that of their trading partners; they subject themselves to various targets and conditions set by lenders. As a result, the ability of governments to compensate the losers and, more broadly, to manage social tensions is greatly curtailed, while the scope of decisions controlled by the democratic process is reduced by the international economic and political integration. And this combination of an increasing inequality with a reduced sovereignty is likely to exacerbate social conflicts and weaken the nascent democratic institutions.

A Preview: The State, Democracy, and the Economy

Is this road to the First World the only alternative available to the less developed countries, East and South? Is this strategy viable economically? Will it be supported by local political forces in the presence of massive dislocations caused by the transformation of economic structures and the ensuing social costs? What kind of cultural forces, nationalistic or religious, is this strategy likely to unleash? Where is it likely to end up, economically and politically? What kind of an international order is it likely to result in? What will happen if and when these strategies fail to generate prosperity and democracy? These are the questions that occupy the rest of this book.

Most of these questions entail the relation between economic and political reforms. Since transitions to democracy often coincide with economic crises, many new democracies face simultaneously an urgent need to consolidate the nascent political institutions and to overcome the economic collapse. Democratic institutions can be consolidated only if they offer the politically relevant groups the appropriate channels and incentives to process their demands within the framework of representative institutions. Yet the reforms necessary to restore the capacity to grow inevitably engender a transitional deterioration of the material conditions of many groups. Hence, consolidation of democratic institutions can be easily undermined under such conditions. This is the source of the dilemma faced by many new democracies: how to create incentives for political forces to process their interests within the democratic institutions while undertaking economic reforms that cause a transitional decline of material welfare? The question thus arises whether there is any reform strategy that would simultaneously lead to resumed growth and strengthen democracy.[14]

This is the central question that motivates this inquiry. What we want to know is what makes democratic institutions work and last, what makes democracy "sustainable"? By "work," we mean that they generate normatively desirable and politically desired effects, such as economic growth, material security, freedom from arbitrary violence, and other conditions conducive to the full development of individuals. By "last," we mean that they absorb and effectively regulate all major conflicts, that rules are changed only according to rules. And while empirical evidence is scant, there are grounds to believe that democracies that work, at least in the economic realm, are more likely to last. Between 1951 and 1988 among the countries with a per capita income of $5,000[15] or less, democracies that grew confronted a 4.2 percent chance of not surviving during the current year, while those that did not grow faced a 9.6 percent chance of falling. In confirmation of Lipset's (1960) hypothesis, the poorest democracies were most sensitive to economic performance: among the countries with a per capita income below $1,000, those that grew had a 96.7 percent chance of surviving, while those that did not confronted only an 81.0 percent chance (Przeworski and Limongi 1993). In turn, Edward Muller (1988) found that democracies are highly sensitive to income inequality.

What, then, are the conditions under which democracies work and last? While our answers range broadly, most of our analysis focuses on the role of the state. The focus on regimes and on markets during the past fifteen years or so suffered from a flagrant omission. In particular, it took O'Donnell's (1992) paper to remind us that we have become blinded to the state, an almost exclusive earlier fixation of researchers and politicians. Yet without an effective state, there can be no democracy and no markets. And, as O'Donnell has shown, the effect of democratization on political and economic conditions is contingent on the institutional viability and the effectiveness of state institutions. Hence, while we share the widespread agreement that in several countries the state has become too large, politically onerous, and economically inefficient, we are alarmed by the antistatist bias of the current reforms. Indeed, in our view the principal mistake of neoliberal prescriptions is that they underestimate the role of state institutions in organizing both the public and the private life of groups and individuals. If democracy is to be sustained, the state must guarantee territorial integrity and physical security, it must maintain the conditions necessary for an effective exercise of citizenship, it must mobilize public savings, coordinate resource allocation, and correct income distribution. And if state institutions are to be capable of performing these tasks, they must be reorganized, rather than simply reduced. Hence, our main concern throughout is to assess the proper role of the state in the political as well as the economic realms. Our arguments about the state concern its role in preserving territorial integrity, in providing conditions for an effective exercise of democratic citizenship, in assuring a modicum of material security, and in allocating economic resources.

The question concerning the role of the state in preserving territorial integrity is raised by the recent events in the former Soviet Union and former Yugoslavia: why do some multinational states survive the collapse of the authoritarian regime while others do not? Except in Spain, democratization occurred until recently in countries where the integrity of the state was not problematic. The breakup of the Soviet Union, Yugoslavia, and Czechoslovakia raises a new set of issues because there democratization unleashed movements for national independence; indeed, for some political forces, democratization is synonymous with national self-determination and the breakdown of the multinational state that was maintained by authoritarian rule. Under such conditions, Hobbes's first problem – how to avoid being killed by others – is logically and historically prior to his second problem – how to prevent people within the same community from killing one another. This is the topic of Chapter 1.

The state is essential in creating the conditions for the effective exercise of citizenship for all members of a political community. Democracy is a system of rights and responsibilities, but the conditions necessary to exercise them are not automatically generated by the mere existence of democratic institutions: a viable state is necessary to make their exercise possible. Hence, the question of the relation between the state, citizenship, and democracy is again prior to the analysis of democracy per se. This question is the subject of Chapter 2.

Democracies are not all the same. Systems of representation, arrangements of division and supervision of powers, manners of organization of interests, legal doctrines, as well as bundles of rights and obligations associated with citizenship differ significantly across regimes that are generally recognized as democratic. These differences, expressed in minute institutional features, generate in their combination emergent effects that, in spite of two thousand years of reflection and investigation, we still understand poorly. We are still far from robust answers to the question posed in 1771 by Rousseau in his *Constitution of Poland*: what institutions have which effects under which historical conditions? Chapter 3 reviews the current state of knowledge concerning this question.

The viability and the effect of institutions depend on the political and cultural conditions under which they emerge and function. Chapter 4 presents the conjecture that several of the conditions that are generally thought to have sustained democratic institutions in the countries where they are by now well established are absent in the new democracies.

Hence, Part I is organized as follows. Since the issues pertaining to the state are logically prior to those concerning the political regime, conditions for preserving territorial integrity are analyzed in Chapter 1, followed by a discussion of the relation between the state, citizenship, and democracy in Chapter 2. In Chapter 3, the analysis then shifts to the effects of specific systems of democratic institutions and in Chapter 4 to the political and cultural context in which these institutions function in new democracies.

Part II extends the analysis to economic issues. The fall of communism in Eastern Europe and the Soviet Union, occurring as the *coup de grace* in a decade of increasingly neoliberal economic policies in capitalist countries, has generated a widespread belief that the only viable economic model is capitalism as we have known it. Yet, although in the first moments of the anticommunist euphoria, the model to follow seemed predetermined and obvious, the issues of the role of the state versus markets, of forms of property, and of development strategies do not and will not go away. "Moving in the direction of 'normal' economies," "embracing the model tested by the historical experience of the developed countries," "constructing a market economy like in the West," and other similar formulae are not sufficient to guide the economic transformations, either in the East or the South, since "normal" economies differ greatly in the degree of state intervention, in the organization of firms, industries, financial institutions, and collective bargaining systems, as well as in social welfare provision. Imitating the United States does not point one in the same direction as followed by Sweden or Japan. Moreover, it is not at all certain that the alternatives facing Eastern Europe are indeed limited to those already tested elsewhere. First, some kind of a reformed state sector is likely to continue producing most of the national product in these countries within the foreseeable future. Second, the sentiments for some kind of a workers' self- management system remain strong.[16]

We challenge the view that the only alternative to communism is either the absence of government intervention or the massive privatization of public enterprises. The conventional belief in the efficiency of capitalism, understood as a combination of a reliance on markets with private ownership of the productive resources, is based on the belief that (1) competitive markets are sufficient to generate efficiency and (2) private property rights provide the correct incentives and information to economic agents. Yet it is well known that the market mechanism fails in cases of (positive or negative) externalities in production and consumption, public goods, and information and transaction costs that make the existence of some markets difficult. To cite Stiglitz (1991: 12), "Adam Smith's invisible hand may be more like the Emperor's new clothes: invisible because it is not there." The notion that, if only left alone, "the market" would efficiently coordinate the allocation of scarce resources, is purely hortatory. In the words of Murrell's (1991: 73) conclusion of his devastating critique of reforms based on the standard neoclassical model, "blanket prescriptions . . . surely do not deserve a place in the debates between economists." And in all capitalist economies, government intervention corrects for these market failures and improves upon the distributional equity of the market-determined allocation.

Clearly, as the debate concerning public goods has shown, the mere fact that "the market does not do it" does not yet imply that the state would do it better. We still need to rethink the role of the state in a decentralized economy in which some markets are inevitably missing and information is imperfect. The danger highlighted by neoliberal economists (Stigler 1975, Tollison 1982) – that the very capacity of the state to engage in productive activities and to favor private projects differentially would cause rent seeking – is real. Hence, the question of how to organize state institutions so that they would engage in activities that are socially beneficial and abstain from responding to private interests remains open. The economic literature concerning the effects of state autonomy on efficiency and growth offers two conflicting perspectives. Recent neoclassical models of regimes (Przeworski 1990, Barro 1991, Findlay 1990, Olson 1991) see any form of state autonomy as causing either an under- or an oversupply of government services. In contrast, some empirical studies see the key to development in "the ability of the state to insulate economic management from the pressure of short-run rent-seeking by powerful interest groups" (Bardhan 1988: 137; see also Haggard 1990). Yet, however this controversy is resolved, the answer that the state should be prevented from any discretionary intervention, limiting its role to promoting the "freedom of individual enterprise," is simply insufficient. Problems of institutional design cannot be avoided by throwing the state out of the economy. They must be confronted as such.

The reason is that institutional questions are not limited to the role of "the state." Any capitalist economy, in which markets are inevitably incomplete and particular economic agents have access to different information, comprises several relations between principals and agents: managers and employees, owners and managers, creditors and entrepreneurs, citizens and politicians. The performance of firms, and of the economy as a whole, depends on the design of institutions that regulate these relations. What matters is whether the employees have incentives and can be monitored to maximize effort, whether managers have incentives and can be monitored to maximize profits, and whether the state has incentives and can be monitored not to respond to pressures by special interests. The very language of "the market" subject to "intervention" obscures real issues: the problem we face is not of the market versus the state but of specific institutional mechanisms that would provide particular economic agents, including the state, with incentives and information that would lead them to behave in collectively rational manners.

The generic issues concern the role of the state in coordinating resource allocation, the welfare and distributional properties of alternative structures of ownership, and development strategies, if any. These problems have a long history, which we need not reproduce here. We concentrate only on questions that are of a current practical significance in the East and the South.

Market-oriented reforms are the subject of Chapter 5. We argue that these reforms should be judged by their success in reviving growth under democratic institutions and define the central dilemma they pose in new democracies. We then review the empirical support for the three central hypotheses that organize our analysis and draw policy consequences from this analysis. Our approach calls for orienting reforms toward growth, for protecting material welfare against the transitional effects of reforms, and for making full use of democratic institutions in the formulation and implementation of reform policies. Yet the dynamic of market-oriented reforms is still poorly understood, in part because of the paucity of successful experiences. Hence, our intent is not to provide comparable inductive evidence for each of the points: this is simply not feasible at the present. Nor is it to develop a blueprint for a policy that could be applied everywhere: reform strategies must trade off conflicting objectives to meet constraints that are specific to each situation. Yet we do argue that several trade-offs – notably between stabilization and growth, between social expenditures and growth, between social expenditures and the sustainability of reforms, and between political participation and the sustainability of reforms – are misconceived within the model that underlies the currently fashionable policy prescriptions.

While we recognize that competitive markets are necessary to achieve an efficient and vigorous economy, we challenge the view that full-scale private ownership is indispensable for guaranteeing incentives for the efficient use of productive assets. Although the privatization of public enterprises constitutes an integral part of standard prescriptions for market-oriented reforms, it raises distinct issues. In Chapter 6 we point out the pitfalls of large-scale privatization and present the argument that viable alternatives to privatization do exist.

Finally, in the Conclusion we collect the different threads in an attempt to identify the dangers facing new democracies and the conditions under which democracy can be sustained in those countries that have recently experienced a political transition and an economic crisis.

Part I
DEMOCRACY AND DEMOCRATIC INSTITUTIONS

1. Transitions to Democracy and Territorial Integrity

Democratization is often considered inherently more difficult in multinational states than in polities in which all people see themselves as members of the same community. Under conditions of shared membership, it is presumed, the principle of shared institutions is not contested; the only issue is the structure of the institutions that are to be shared. The classic statement of this view is that of John Stuart Mill, who in his *Considerations on Representative Government* (1958: 230) argued: "Free institutions are next to impossible in a country made up of different nationalities. Among a people without fellow-feeling, especially if they read and speak different languages, the united public opinion, necessary to the working of representative government, cannot exist." Similarly, Robert Dahl (1971: 110–111) reasoned that nationality differences within states restricted participation for some citizens, thereby limiting the possibility for a successful polyarchy. His empirical data gave support to his reasoning; among 114 polities, 58 percent with a low degree of subcultural pluralism, 36 percent with moderate pluralism, and only 15 percent with marked pluralism were polyarchies, or nearly so.

Alvin Rabushka and Kenneth Shepsle (1972) provided microfoundations for these views. They argued that in plural societies political entrepreneurs, through the use of ambiguity, can win votes among all ethnic groups. Politicians who give ambiguous messages are in essence offering the voters a lottery. And, even if voters have intense preferences in favor of their own group's interests, they would prefer a lottery in which their first preference has a small possibility to a sure promise of a moderate policy in favor of their own group. Therefore, politicians can construct broad-based multiethnic coalitions. But the lottery solution is not stable, especially in the case of postcolonial democracies where multiethnic coalitions were based on broad anticolonial platforms. Once independence is achieved, political entrepreneurs from each community recognize that the multiethnic coalitions were oversized and surmise that they can defeat the coalition within their own community by advocating extreme positions. This "outbidding" polarizes the polity. In turn, the winner of an election in which each cultural group is promised political dominance is likely to so oppress the losers as to induce violence, civil war, and a breakdown of democracy. There is, then, for Rabushka and Shepsle, a rational logic of breakdown in multinational democratic systems.

The theoretical problem with the thesis that multinational states have greater difficulties in reaching democratic outcomes is that these authors assume that ethnic identity is "primordially given." Primordialist theory assumes that people are born into particular cultural identities and that their deepest commitments and most strongly held values are determined by the inherited identities. Serbs murder Croats because of the centuries-long antipathies between these peoples; once born a Serb, you inherit an antagonistic stance toward Croats. Harry Eckstein (1966: 34) adopts the primordialist viewpoint when he holds that ethnic and cultural cleavages are more "objective" than those of interest group or class. He deduces from this observation that while social mobility may be possible, cultural mobility is not. Primordialists can thereby explain the intensity of feeling and the intractability of political conflict over cultural issues.

In direct contradiction to primordialists, much recent scholarship has demonstrated that common cultural roots are neither a necessary nor a sufficient condition for ethnic or national membership. Nations are not direct descendants of ancient families who establish a historic right to rule in modern clothes; rather they are modern political movements that rely on myths of common ancestry in order to legitimate their domination over society through the means of a state apparatus.[17] Because minuscule cultural differences can be magnified and reified as part of a political process, most states encompass populations whose members could, if circumstances warrant, declare themselves distinct culturally, linguistically, or religiously from other people who live within the same boundaries. And since ethnic identity is manipulable and changing, as Robert Bates (1983) and many others have shown, the constructions of similarity and difference must be explained as an outcome, not taken as a given. Somalia is a distressing but exemplary case. A tyrant in this linguistically, religiously, and culturally homogeneous country was overthrown in 1991; the opposition forces divided themselves into an interclan and even intraclan civil war. And the rhetoric of the interclan battle was one of national differences.

Although theoretically discredited, primordialist theory reemerged phoenix-like from the collapse of the communist order in Eastern Europe. We now read that the Serbs and Croats are returning to their natural antipathies, after being held back from one another by a police state. But we should ask why are the irreconcilable differences rather than the immense similarities of these two peoples politically salient at this time? Surely, the objective differences between them are no greater than those between Normans and Bretons, between Bavarians and Rhinelanders, or between Piedmontese and Sicilians. If people within a polity emphasize their cultural differences and engage in ethnic outbidding, it is more likely a consequence of institutional failure rather than a cause of it.

To be sure, the historical construction of Slovaks, Slovenians, and Kazaks means that members of these groups have a clear sense of their "real" identities, and so they are easily mobilizable on the bases of these shared identities. These historically constructed national communities must be studied in their own right. Countries that have more than one such community (the former Czechoslovakia) will face different challenges in democratic transitions than those countries that do not (Poland). But historical construction implies the possibility of contemporary deconstruction. Any theory about multinationalism that fails to provide a dynamic for changing identities will miss crucial aspects of transitional politics.

The empirical problem with the thesis of the instability of democracy in multinational polities is that once the age of a country is taken into account, the striking support that Dahl has found begins to dissipate.[18] A significant percentage of states that received independence in the post–World War II era in South Asia and Africa were governed in the colonial period in such a way as to emphasize the cultural differences of the peoples within each polity's borders. There are very few cases of democracy in these countries. But among the old states, the relationship is at best weak: Belgium, Canada, Spain, and Switzerland are multinational democracies; China is an autocracy with no significant nationality issue (at least in the eastern part of the country, with 95 percent of the population); and Germany, Japan, and Italy, none of which faced internal nationality divisions, were the three most significant democratic failures in the 1930s, when all democracies were in peril.

Furthermore, there is no systematic evidence that the mobilization of nationalities within states occurs more often in periods of democratization than at other times. Regional revivals in Spain and the former Czechoslovakia occurred during periods of democratization but similar revivals in Quebec and Flanders occurred in countries that were already stable democracies. A compelling explanation for nationalistic revivals, offered by Peter Gourevitch (1979), is that they occur in periods of institutional decline at the center or economic dynamism in a culturally peripheral region. When regional interests see declining resources in the center, they will seek to mobilize the masses of their region to separate from that center – and the best way to mobilize regional masses is to appeal to a common culture that unites them in the region and differentiates them from the center. Nationalist ideologies fill that bill.

If relative overdevelopment creates incentives for one type of regional revival, relative underdevelopment unleashes an analogous process. National movements in relatively deprived regions such as Tatary and Abkhazia coincided with processes of democratization, but movements in Bangladesh and Kosovo did not. If the collapse of authoritarianism unleashes regional revival movements, this is due not to democratization per se but to the weakness of the center amidst the process. The general point holds: regionally based nationalisms do not cause institutional failure at the center; rather, institutional failure at the center provides a context in which regionally based nationalists can effectively mobilize to promote an autonomy movement. In light of the theoretical and empirical difficulties of the theses connecting multinationalism with democratic failure or democratization with ethnic arousal, the presupposition that multinationalism poses extraordinary problems in redemocratization needs to be reappraised.

We turn now to a more positive approach: how the emergence of international conflicts in the process of democratization has been, and can be, resolved. A subfield of political science has addressed itself to the problem of designing political institutions that can withstand the politicization of cultural differences. Political institutions in Belgium, Spain, and Nigeria are notable in their ability to frame national conflicts in non-zero-sum bargaining games.

Lijphart (1977) and many others outlined an institutional design of "consociational democracy" that is sharply different from majoritarian democracy. The institutional key to consociational democracy is the recognition of diverse "segments," where the leaders of each segment serve in a grand coalition (much like Plato's "nocturnal council"), and each has a right to veto any proposed legislation. Each segment has as well a right to a proportional share of civil service appointments and seats in the parliament. Finally, each segment is given a high degree of autonomy in running its internal affairs, especially those concerning education, religion, and culture.

There are many criticisms of the applicability of consociational theory to the processes of democratization. For one, the model has not done well when cultural cleavages become very sharp. Where sharp cleavages lead people to think the benefits of cooperation are declining, vetoes become endemic, and the resultant stagnation provides proof of the failure of the consociational system. Lijphart's seminal work was a study of consociation in the Netherlands, a country where cleavages were never as sharply politicized as they have been, say, in Lebanon or South Africa, where Lijphart has sought to apply his model.[19] Second, one can question the degree to which consociation is democratic when political leaders have virtual control over their segments (Lustick 1979). Third, consociational models tend to break down when the population balance changes, especially when the natural increase of the lower class is higher than that of the upper class, or when employers recruit foreign labor. Few countries can maintain population ratios that are reflective of bargains made generations earlier. Switzerland has, but only by excluding migrant workers from its polity.

It would be foolhardy, however, to ignore the issues of institutional design raised by the consociational school. Perhaps most important are the various insights with regard to proportional representation and other voting mechanisms. For example, the voting formula for the Nigerian second republic induced ethnic groups to build coalitions across regions (Dudley 1982). The failure of the Second Republic was perhaps overdetermined, but it is significant that ethnic/cultural tensions were not part of the explanation. Donald Horowitz's (1991) institutional recommendation for South Africa is not consociational, yet it does take into account the incentives for party leaders to build coalitions across ethnic boundaries rather than emphasize cultural differences.

Not only electoral design but also, as Linz and Stepan (1992) demonstrate, the sequencing of institutions and elections may have important implications for the scale and intensity of ethnic political claims. In Spain after Franco's death, although there was strong regional consciousness, local elites did not have the resources to organize elections in a preemptive move to counteract the reform program designed by actors committed to the integrity of the central state. Adolfo Suárez, appointed by the king to guide Spain's democratic transition, wisely called for all-Spain elections to approve the law for political reform and to select representatives to a constituent assembly. These elections preceded regional ones, thereby creating an incentive for people to join central parties. Another consequence of this order is that the writing of the constitution preceded the discussion of autonomy statutes. Thus, the writing of those statutes had to be placed within the context of a Spanish-wide fundamental law, already legitimitized by elections. In contrast, in the transitions that took place in the former Soviet Union and former Yugoslavia, regional forces had the institutional resources to call for elections that preempted all-union elections. Linz and Stepan (1992: 134) note that "virtually the day after the regional elections (in the Soviet Union and Yugoslavia) the statewide legitimacy of the central government was damaged because the nationalist regional forces could make a stronger claim to democratic legitimacy via elections.'' Under such a context, when regional politicians were democratically elected but central politicians were not, the 9+1 negotiations in the Soviet Union were undermined by the intensity of regionalist pressures. Further study is clearly needed to specify the degree of freedom of elites to order the sequencing of elections and of institutions. But the record shows that if choice is available, the sequence from all-union to region, in elections and in basic law, bodes better for democracy.

Closely related to issues of electoral formulae are those of party formation. National parties that seek to build alliances that crosscut cultural groups in all regions tend to modulate the demands from regionally based autonomy movements. That the two ruling centralist parties (UCD and PSOE) in democratic Spain never sought support exclusively within the non-autonomist constituencies in Catalonia and Basque Country meant that there was space for Catalans and Basques with good regionalist credentials to join centralist parties or coalitions.[20] In Nigeria, the constitutional drafters recognized this issue and required that to become accredited parties must have significant membership across a variety of regions. The structure of party competition, then, affects the viability of democracy in multiethnic states.

Those who propose institutional designs to limit the exacerbation of nationality conflicts in the process of democratization presuppose that different sectors of the society agree about the threat to the center that is entailed by demands for regional autonomy. They also assume that political leaders can coordinate successfully on a common set of political institutions that are designed to minimize that threat. A typical example of this genre is Gunther, Sani, and Shabad's (1986) discussion of the Spanish transition. Undoubtedly leaders of all parties, with their common memories of the civil war and their intense desire for Spain to become part of Europe, had an incentive to search for an agreement that would limit the range of political competition. This helps explain the willingness of party leaders in Spain to seek a pact. But it does not explain why the pact was reached. Game theory teaches us that a common desire by contesting parties to reach a superior equilibrium is insufficient to explain how such an equilibrium is reached. Coordination over institutional design is a strategic problem that students of pacts have largely ignored. Yet to attain political pacts (whether they be implicit or explicit) that enhance the chances for the survival of democracy in the face of actual and potential claims for autonomy, political leaders and their constituents must solve a variety of strategic problems.

Game theoretic models can help in the analysis of these strategic problems.

To develop such models, it is important to specify the "players" who are involved. The "state" (sometimes called "the center" and other times "the ruler") is the central apparatus that is interested in the effective administration of law. Within the state there are interests that compete for control over the state apparatus. These interests share a vision of the state as already having legitimate boundaries and a common national membership. A "regional elite" is that set of political leaders who contest the vision of the centralized state and have an interest in the decentralization of state authority. "Regional revival movements" occur when this elite mobilizes the masses within the region in the name of a common nationality, in order to build a political constituency for political autonomy.[21] The regional elite, however, is not a unified set of actors; different segments will have different satisfaction points on the road from centralization to regional sovereignty. Another key set of actors in the games that follow is the "people." Those people who define themselves as culturally from the region face important choices, for example, in regard to complying with new regional laws that require their children to be educated in the language of the region. Those people who identify themselves culturally with the center but live in the region where a revival movement is taking place face choices as to whether to assimilate into the culture of the region, to emigrate, or to seek protection within the region. Finally, "vigilantes" are that subset of people who identify culturally with the region and who organize themselves to promote and protect that culture. They see themselves as providing a "collective good" to the region by pressing for universal adoption of the regional language and other regional cultural forms, even if it is in the private interest of most people from the region not to adopt these forms.

The overriding strategic problem for both representatives of the state and those of a culturally distinct region within that state is one of making credible commitments in the form of threats and promises. Four distinct strategic issues are involved. First, rulers want to establish a reputation for being able to authoritatively allocate resources in the society. To do this, they must make a credible threat to regionalists that the center will not quickly or easily cave in to demands for secession. Second, rulers will want to be able to make a credible promise that if the regional leaders accept early concessions for devolution of power, the center will not take advantage of the ensuing political quiescence of the region to build up sufficient strength to recentralize the polity. Third, regional activists will want to make a credible threat that if there is no devolution of power to the region, a civil war might follow. Fourth, regional leaders will need to make a credible promise that if they receive autonomy, they will not use their new power to escalate demands (for complete sovereignty) or to maltreat minorities within their region (especially those of the same ethnic/national group as the political center).

Let us begin with credible threats by rulers. Why should a state resist when facing nationalist demands for autonomy or sovereignty (e.g., Slovakia, Slovenia, Croatia, the former Soviet Union republics in the 9+1 negotiations, Catalonia, Basque Country, Quebec)? Leaving aside the franquist-type claim of "the idea of Spain," which evokes images of states having souls, one important reason has to do with the establishment of the center's reputation for the making of credible threats against attacks on its integrity. Suppose a regional elite makes a demand for autonomy, and the center accedes to this demand. Invariably, politicians in other regions will feel pressures from their own constituencies to make parallel demands. For example, it could be argued that to keep up with Catalonia and Basque Country, Galicia received more autonomy than it would have otherwise wanted, or that Uzbekistan's claims for independence were based on a feeling that it should get at least what the Baltic states were demanding. While a state may be able to handle administratively the separation of a region, a succession of such administrative procedures, coming from a ramifying set of smaller and smaller regions, will without doubt consume the administrative capacity of central elites. (Anyone who has observed Nigeria moving from three regions to twelve states in 1967, to thirty-one states in 1991, will have a good idea of the process.) Endless haggling over transfers of services and property can easily undermine the capacity of the government to rule. Central rulers therefore have an interest in resisting early demands for autonomy, even if those demands have good reason behind them, for fear of evoking a whole series of demands (from regions with less cause for seeking autonomy) that would hinder successful governance. Building a reputation early for being resistant to such demands will teach leaders of smaller regions to hold back their demands, and perhaps to accommodate themselves to central rule.

Rulers must also worry about their reputation with their own repressive and administrative apparatus. If they yield to ever increasing autonomy demands, military elites who see themselves as protecting the unity of the state and administrative elites who have secure jobs administering state programs in the region will feel threatened. The breakdown of state order, or the planning of a coup d'état, both of which threaten democracy, could result. Thus, fear of subversion by their own agents is yet another reason why rulers will want to resist demands for regional autonomy. Of course, a militant strategy by a state seeking to maintain its reputation could backfire. But reputation must be taken into account when considering the possibility of institutional pacts that permit autonomy to culturally distinct regions.

The state also needs to make – here is the second strategic issue – credible promises to regional negotiators not to rescind concessions after regaining sufficient coercive, economic, and administrative power that would enable it to undermine the separatist threat. If this promise is not credible, regional actors will reject concessions that stop short of complete independence. One way to make these promises credible is to provide ''hostages'' (in this case control over state resources) that would enable regional actors to withstand future efforts at recentralization. Intense bargaining in Spain in the 1980s on the question of whether regions should be funded through transfers from centrally collected taxes or through taxation within the autonomous regions was partly driven on regional fears that Madrid had designs for recentralization. Transfers were more efficient but direct taxing power in the regions provides ''hostages'' to regional authorities. In the 9+1 negotiations in the Soviet Union, Gorbachev was unable to make a credible promise that a resurgent Moscow would not seek to undermine concessions to the union republics, and this may partly explain the failure of those negotiations.

The third strategic issue is that of regional activists trying to make a credible threat that they can cause trouble for the regime if it denies them some level of autonomy. One way to do this is to permit, even encourage, rabid nationalists from within the society to engage in low-scale civil war (or vigilante action) to terrorize those people who do not demonstrate regional solidarity. Vigilante groups in support of regional sovereignty often form autonomously in the rural heartland of the regional culture, and they need little encouragement to terrorize central police and other representatives of the state. These vigilantes are often especially brutal to members of the regional culture who serve as representatives of the central state. By encouraging such groups over which they have only minimal control, regional leaders are demonstrating a commitment to autonomy that they themselves will find difficult to back out of. These threats, in that they ''leave something to chance'' (Schelling 1963: Chap. 8), become credible. That is to say, by risking repression by the center, regional leaders signal the intensity of their preferences.

The fourth strategic issue and one at the heart of the regionalist strategy is not that of credible threats, however, but of credible promises. Suppose that a region makes a demand for autonomy in regard to education and environment, and the center wants to be sure that, if it accedes, it will not be faced with future demands for regional control over taxation and currency.

Can a regional elite make a credible promise? The central government may surmise that if the regional elites with whom it bargains hold to that commitment, the government will be undermined by competitors seeking to make the original bargain obsolescent. When the two Germanys united, radical Catalanists and Basques excoriated their own regional leadership for not getting as good a bargain as was now permissible in Europe. Many called for the undermining of the status quo. Only the impressive economic boom in northern Spain put a damper on those claims.

Another issue of credible promises by regional leaders, and one with far bloodier implications, concerns those regions in which (politically or demographically) significant pockets of the population identify themselves as coming from the center: Serbs in Croatia, Hindus in those parts of India that were slated to become Pakistan, Russians in Moldova and Ukraine, Protestants in Northern Ireland, Turks in Cyprus, Pieds Noirs in Algeria, whites in Rhodesia, and Afrikaners in Azania. This phenomenon has been identified in the literature as one of "settler colonialism." Settler colonialism is a subtype of the nationality issue that entails the intractable problem of boundaries that can never adequately encompass an entire nationality group while at the same time excluding nonmembers of that nationality. To the extent that these settlers feel protected by the central state and potentially threatened by the regional one, the granting of regional autonomy has ominous implications. The strategic problem for regional elites is how to make a credible commitment that the settlers would be protected under their rule. If, under the ancien regime, the central police force (or other agents of the center) terrorized the regional population, then as that regime begins to collapse, people who lost friends and relatives to the terror will seek revenge. That revenge is most easily vented on the settler population, whether or not it was implicated in the terror. In turn, fearful of retribution, the settlers will seek to portray the regional elites as unable to protect them; they will seek to undermine any pact for regional autonomy. If they incite violence, the police forces of the center will have to protect life and property; but by so doing, conflicts between center and region will be exacerbated, undermining negotiations for a pact.

Not only settlers, but all minority populations within regions, will distrust regional commitments to provide them with basic protection. South Ossetians in Georgia, for example, sent in 1991–1992 delegations to Russia urging President Yeltsin to maintain Community of Independent States troops in their region to defend them against Georgian nationalists. The more that regional elites articulate their desire for separation in nationalist terms, the more the minority populations will feel politically excluded and physically threatened in the new order. The basic question is then, How can regional elites make claims for national separation and commitments to protect minorities at the same time?

A prominent concern in the making of credible promises by regional leaders is that of policing the vigilantes, who in the name of the national project, may overlook the democratic rights of individuals within the region, including the rights of those who identify themselves culturally with the region yet have political and economic connections with the center. While living under centralized rule, some people pursue their interests through compromise with the regime. They learn the central language and enter into various networks with the center. Suppose a regional autonomy movement (as in Basque Country) makes demands that all education must be conducted in the regional language. Given the alternative between centralization (in which everyone is educated in the language of the center) and autonomy (in which everyone is educated in the language of the region), most voters are likely to perceive the latter as the better alternative and vote for it. Yet if the regional alternative wins, many voters may subvert that program in their private lives, since many people (in this case even those articulating the demands) who consider themselves cultural regionalists cannot communicate effectively in the regional language and fear that their children may become too provincial if they were educated through the regional medium. As can be demonstrated through a Schelling (1978: chap. 7) tipping model, in the early stages of the regional revival of languages, it would be irrational for each family to enroll its child in a regional-language school (see Laitin 1989). It would only be rational to do so if a significant percentage of the population already complied with the regional program. Regional activists seeking autonomy therefore must assure the population that the private subverters of the regional program will not undermine the movement toward a full cultural revival. They do this, at least to some degree, through vigilante action. By policing cheaters, as well as through public excoriation, humiliation (and in the Basque case), terror and forced taxation, they raise the costs of subverting the regional program. Yet they also deny individuals in their region basic democratic rights.

Vigilante policing also endangers democratization because it involves violence. Regional violence, in turn, attracts central police forces. Vigilantes have an interest in a myth that regional unity is being subverted not from within but from without. They will therefore blame the violence neither on their activities, nor on the subverters of their program from within the region, but on the intimidation by central police authorities. This process can lead to a spiral of regional–centrist violence.

Terrorism is only one tactic used by vigilantes to dispirit and threaten the military and administrative representatives of the central state. They also use terror to discourage people from their region who defy the regional autonomy program. There is no adequate theory telling us the conditions under which such a tactic is likely to be used. But once it is used, a double mechanism operates to sustain it. First, the gains from terror (the ransom given by an industrialist to free his son from captivity, the capture of explosives from an army base, the murder of a local politician associated with a centrist party) are tangible and spectacular. Vigilante leaders become slaves to a "tyranny of small victories." They may lose popular support through their gory acts; the great majority of the people in the region may give their moral support to moderates who seek compromises through negotiation. But the small spectacular victories can become, for terrorists, compelling evidence of imminent independence.[22] Second, regional terror invites into the region the security forces from the center. To the extent that central police seek to protect all citizens, they become targets of the terror. Vigilante terror spirals into guerilla warfare.

None of these four commitment problems is easy to solve, and solving one (e.g., regional leaders engaging in a form of brinkmanship by allowing nationalist vigilantes free to roam the streets and terrorize minorities) may vitiate the solution to another (regional leaders making a credible promise to the center that they will stop vigilantes from terrorizing minorities). It is a complex political task to encourage and control terrorism at the same time.

Examining pressures for national autonomy in strategic terms helps to reemphasize the point that national groups are political constructions, not primordial givens. To be sure, the strategic problems are thorny ones, but less thorny than if we assumed that all cultural groups were primordially real. Certain implications follow from this point.

The first implication is that it would be a mistake to reify these groups by acknowledging their monopoly rights to a historic homeland. To do so would be to imply that Turks in Germany, Russians in Estonia, Ossetians in Georgia, and Algerians in France have their political rights restricted because they inhabited a region at a later historical period than the ancestors of the so-called autochthonous population. To acknowledge the right of Crimean Tatars to return to their homeland from which they were inhumanely displaced is not to acknowledge the illegitimacy of the Ukrainian population that lives in the Crimea today. Central states must, given the present configuration of interests, devolve power to regional groups. But this devolution should be legally based on territorial notions of membership rather than a criterion of "historical communities." While the same amount of power can be devolved, doing so on territorial grounds, rather than those of historical community rights, compels regional elites to accept the responsibility of providing citizenship rights to their own minorities.

The second implication of the denial of primordial reality to national groups is that it would be an error to give specified regional groups enumerated constitutional rights. Rather, group and regional boundaries can be set in the political process and can then be recognized in law. This construction will allow for changing definitions of the group to be accommodated without constitutional change, implying that the political process that created autonomous regions can be used by all political forces to redefine the boundaries of the region or to eliminate those boundaries should assimilation with the majority population occur. The Spanish constitution provides a framework for the process of creating autonomies, but does not mention any particular autonomy. Thus, no potential autonomy gets slighted, and the specification of autonomous groups is made part of the normal politics of law rather than the extraordinary politics of constitutional change. In India, the constitutional specification of protected languages did not provide much additional protection, yet it angered those groups whose languages were omitted from the list. While this specification did not destroy Indian democracy, it put an unnecessary burden on the democratic state.

A third implication of the denial of primordialism is that people can and often do have multiple identities. It is not a contradiction that 73 percent of Catalans claim to be "proud" of being Spanish, while 82 percent claim to be "proud" to be Catalan, and 83 percent want to be members of a European community (Linz and Stepan 1992: 128). A political process that makes claims on people's complex identities is one in which nationality politics can be played without the spiraling of demands or the competitive outbidding that Rabushka and Shepsle saw as necessary to multinational democratic polities. Under certain conditions appeals to national membership can be seen as part of normal politics, not that of violence and civil wars. The denial of primordial theory allows us to overcome a liberal prejudice, perhaps associated with Dahl's writings, that the national issue must be solved before normal democratic politics can take place. Identity politics under conditions of multiple identities can be as "normal" (i.e., conflictual without revolutionary implications) as Przeworski and Wallerstein's (1982) version of class politics.

And as with class politics, it is incumbent on policy analysts to see the logic of the conflict of interest between the parties, in this case the state and regional elites. In regard to the state, it is crucial to recognize that standing firm against maximalist regionalist demands (as did President Havel in regard to Slovakia and Prime Minister Suárez in regard to Catalonia and Basque Country) should not be considered as fighting a rearguard battle against national liberation. States have a reputation to uphold in order to set limits on a possible cascade of autonomy claims. Nonetheless (as indeed Havel and Suárez recognized), when the center is weak in the process of democratic transition, the state cannot avoid negotiating with regional elites. In turn, regional elites who seek a democratic future must make commitments not to escalate if earlier demands are met, to observe the rights of minorities within their boundaries, to respect property rights of "settler" minorities, and finally to police their own maximalists. Such commitments are not easily established and maintained. Schelling (1963) has written about the possibilities of bargaining impasses in similar situations. Working out the problems of simultaneous commitments by regional and state elites in the context of democratization remains a challenge to both politicians and scholars in the coming years.

The general theme should be clear: despite a generation of research discrediting primordialism as applied to Africa and Asia, the collapse of Soviet hegemony and the rise of nationalist movements brought primordialist arguments back into respectability. The murders of Croats by Serbs, of Armenians by Azeris, of Ossetians by Georgians, have been taken as somehow "natural." They are not natural and require political explanations. Nationalistic movements that threaten democratization through their appeals for separation are not caused, as primordialist arguments would have it, by cultural differences per se; rather the failure of rule explains the mobilization of cultural groups in the name of nationalism. In periods of democratic transition when the center is weak vis-à-vis culturally distinct regions, demands for autonomy are likely to develop. The task of finding best answers to separatist challenges is of crucial importance if violent conflicts are to be avoided. Such answers can be found both in institutional arrangements and in political strategies. Institutional designs giving scope to regional interests might help keep these issues contained within democratic institutions. Group and regional boundaries should be set in the political process rather than recognized as primordially real. Guarantees of minorities' rights should be established, and mechanisms for supervision should be created. Fiscal policies could be oriented to motivate smaller groups to seek autonomy within, rather than through separation from, the larger unit of an integrating state. The strategic problems associated with simultaneous commitments must be solved. All this means that democracies in multinational states will be different from those in which nationality demands have not been articulated, but it does not mean that culturally or nationally heterogeneous societies are not viable candidates for successful democratization.

2. Democracy, Citizenship, and the State

Modern citizenship entails a bundle of predictable and enforceable rights and obligations for every member of the political community. Democracy and citizenship were coextensive in several nineteenth-century European countries because membership in the political community was restricted by law to those who were independently capable of exercising their political rights and obligations. Only those who fulfilled some social and economic prerequisites for the effective exercise of citizenship – property, income or education – were entitled to these rights. With the advent of universal suffrage, a defining condition of democracy became that all individuals must be empowered to exercise as citizens the same rights and obligations. Yet the difficulty faced by contemporary democratic regimes is that while democracy is a system of positive rights, it does not automatically generate the conditions required for an effective exercise of these rights, as well as obligations. In particular, the material security and education, as well as access to information, necessary to exercise citizenship are not guaranteed to everyone by the mere existence of democratic institutions. Hence, in many countries, some groups remain incapable of exercising their rights and obligations. We face a new monster: democracies without an effective citizenship for large sections of the political community.[23]

Citizenship can be universally exercised only when the normative system is guided by universal criteria, when the rule of law is effectively enforced, when public powers are willing and able to protect rights, and when all individuals enjoy some social and economic prerequisites. And only an effective state can generate the conditions that ensure the universal realization of citizenship (O'Donnell 1992).

Three conditions must be fulfilled by the state for citizenship to be effective under democracy:

1. If the exercise of citizenship is to be predictable, governments and officials must themselves act in accordance with the constitution and the laws.

2. A universalist legal system is a constitutive dimension of the order that the state guarantees for a given territory: it includes the rights and obligations of public law and also the regulation of private or common-law relations.

Only the state that predictably enforces laws can enable peaceful private relations. Hence, the extent to which citizenship rights are implementable and enforceable depends on the quality and the quantity of state presence in private relations. If justice and police systems are to be used as a means of exercising rights and as a system for regulating conflicts, citizens must be assured that they are universally and predictably applied.

3. If everyone is to exercise effectively her or his citizenship rights, the social conditions required for such an exercise of rights must be present. While democracy offers to all the right to be free from arbitrary violence, as well as to form and exchange opinions, the exercise of citizenship is feasible only for those individuals who enjoy some modicum of material security, education, and access to information. The connection between property, education, and citizenship is, of course, an old issue in political thought. The connection between liberty and property was emphasized by the republican tradition in the United States; the connection between the capacity to form political opinions and education goes back to Kant. Indeed, it was precisely the recognition of these connections by liberal thought that served during the nineteenth century to restrict the scope of citizenship to those who were judged to be capacitated to exercise it. But once political rights became universal, a minimum of material security and of enlightenment constituted the necessary conditions for effective citizenship.

Citizens as well as the state have to redefine their roles under democracy. Under authoritarianisms of various kinds, the state could provide benefits to selected groups in a discretionary manner. Individuals did not think in terms of rights: rights were not what mattered, since they could not be exercised and could always be violated. Authoritarian regimes could enforce some rights and violate others: they were arbitrary. Conversely, since the state appeared as an arbitrary power, individuals did not think in terms of civic responsibilities: the language of obligation was used by dictatorships as an instrument of repression. Under democracy, citizens can no longer treat obligations as imposed by a hostile force but as necessitated by the requirements of social cohesion. Non-voting and tax avoidance, widespread in new democracies, debilitate the already frail state. A mutual set of obligations must be defined between the state and the citizenry: If, on the one hand, the state does not enforce the rights and responsibilities of citizenship and if, on the other hand, citizens do not organize to make their rights effective and to compel the state to acquit itself of its responsibilities, the very concept of citizenship is rendered ineffectual.

New democracies have to address simultaneously the civil, political, and social requirements of citizenship. They cannot follow the long experience of Western Europe, where the rule of law, the system of political rights, and the rights to social welfare and education were faced as successive challenges. Yet the current circumstances of regime transitions and economic crises put all these prerequisites of citizenship under pressure in many countries:

1. Concerning constitutionality, many governments claim that given the gravity of the economic crisis, the new democratic governments can renege on their legal, even constitutional commitments. Some of citizens' appeals to the legal system on behalf of their constitutionally guaranteed rights and the judicial verdicts that follow force governments to choose between obeying the constraints of the economic situation or conforming to legality. Under these conditions, many governments seek to rule by exceptional means.

2. In many new democracies, the rule of law is implemented irregularly throughout the territory, while vast social differences exist in the protection of citizenship rights. Ineffective states coexist with autonomous spheres of power: these operate under different rules and often degenerate into systems of private violence and private domination, into familism, regionalism, prebendalism, or personalism; their connections with the state are often based on the exchange of votes, political favors, public funds, and administrative resources. These states can ensure neither the rule of law nor citizenship in important parts of their territories and in large sectors of their societies. In extreme cases, states abandon their law enforcement responsibility for large sectors of the community, whether some parts of the territory, some urban areas, or some social groups. The social and territorial breakup of the public responsibilities of the state is evident not just in the northeast of Brazil and the sierra of Peru, but also in the periphery of many Latin American cities where the state has no effective presence. This includes police protection. In some countries, notably Brazil, the police are so feared that citizens perceive them as a threat rather than as defense. Unequal protection by the state from private violence undermines the very core of citizenship.

3. Education as well as access to basic welfare services are distributed very unequally across social groups. In many countries, basic social services are being de facto privatized or are simply disappearing. In some countries, including Argentina, Brazil, and Poland, whatever effective state bureaucracies and notions of a public-service career that did exist, are being undermined, thus affecting social and territorial homogeneity. Yet the successful cases of democratization, particularly in southern Europe (Maravall 1993),

were precisely those where the state expanded its role as a provider of social protection and of education.

The impact of educational and social inequalities on the exercise of citizenship has been confirmed in a wide range of societies. Lower educational achievement levels are related to greater political skepticism, to pessimism over individuals' personal capacity to influence political decisions or events, to a more limited political participation, and to indifference toward or rejection of democratic politics. Socioeconomic inequalities are also related to such attitudes concerning democratic politics. In Spain, five years after dictatorship had ended, educational inequalities were associated with 25 percentage points of difference in support for democracy, ranges of variation of 1 to 8 percentage points in the distribution of interest towards politics, and of 1 to 10 percentage points in political participation other than the vote (Maravall 1981). In Brazil, by the end of 1989, educational inequalities were reflected in variations of 40 percentage points in interest in politics, and of 28 percentage points in support for democracy (Moisés 1990). In Hungary, social differences were associated with a variation of 37 percentage points in the view that democracy could solve the problems of the country better than dictatorship (Bruszt and Simon 1991). In Poland, 77 percent of respondents with secondary education thought that democracy is the superior form of government and only 48 percent with a primary education held this view (CBOS, July 1993). Since social inequalities turn into political inequalities, the exercise of citizenship rights is affected by differences in social position.

Three reasons may have contributed to this divorce between democracy and effective citizenship:

1. According to the analyses shared across the political spectrum in the mid-1970s (Habermas 1975, Stigler 1975), states in many countries, more and less developed, became victims of invasions by special interests and lost their capacity to pursue universalistic policies. According to these analyses, the state grew too large and distributed too much, thus creating powerful incentives for powerful private groups to pursue their material interests by addressing themselves to the state, rather than to productive activities ("rent seeking"). As a result, not only were states permeated by special interests but they suffered profound fiscal crises. This situation was shared by Latin American as well as Eastern European countries.

2. As we argue later, the effects of these fiscal crises on the state are further aggravated by market-oriented reforms. Stabilization and structural adjustment policies entail recessions and thus reduce the tax base: a phenom-

enon particularly pronounced in Eastern Europe, where the transition to a market economy coincided with the collapse of the Soviet market. Standard adjustment packages often include across-the-board reductions of public spending. Moreover, as in Poland, the erosion of a tax base is frequently aggravated by privatization. And while a reorientation of state activities is inevitable and advisable, indiscriminate cuts of public expenditures reduce the very capacity of the state to guarantee the effective exercise of citizenship rights, particularly in the areas of police protection, education, and income maintenance. Pushed to the extreme, such cuts threaten the very integrity of the state.

3. A more complex hypothesis is that the regime change itself undermines in various ways the viability of states as organizations. We have already seen that in some multinational states, the central bureaucratic apparatus disintegrated as a fiscal, military, and, eventually, political unit. But regime transitions may undermine the viability of the state as an organization even when territorial integrity is not at stake. For one, in countries such as Romania, Albania, and the Philippines, where the previous regime ruled with strong sultanistic tendencies (in the Weberian sense of an extreme form of patrimonialism), their demise left both the state and society disorganized. Second, the distinction made by Fishman (1990) between transitions originating within the state and those within the regime leads us to expect that the state apparatus will be more affected in the former case: a difference between Portugal and Spain. Finally, in several countries, a process that Jon Elster (1992) calls "the backward looking justice of retribution and restitution" is leading to the purge of the former members of the state apparatus. Attempts to seek revenge for past violations of human rights and other excesses of power can undermine a universalistic concept of citizenship.

Since this last issue is a subtle one, we need some distinctions: there is a difference between retribution for specific violations of existing national and international laws and the attempts to deprive some categories of persons associated with the past dictatorships of their citizenship rights on a group basis.

One issue is whether those who committed specific violations of human rights should be punished. The main argument in favor is that such punishment would have a dissuasive effect.[24] The fear that mitigates against such punishment is that the military would step back in to prevent it. But there is also an argument (Delich 1984) that since these crimes were committed by the military as an institution, any prosecution would have to be directed against the military institution as such. Posed in these terms, this argument implies that any action against the military would undermine the defensive capacity of the nation, something no government with a minimal dose of nationalism can afford to do. Clearly, this issue has no general solution: it entails a series of decisions that call for both moral and strategic judgments (Acuña and Smulovitz, 1994). The Argentine government of Raul Alfonsin did end up prosecuting the members of the military junta, while the Chilean government of Patricio Aylwyn did not. Yet the mere revelation of such crimes is not enough: the slogan *"Recordar para no repetir"* is based on a tenuous causal chain. Prosecution, even if followed by a pardon, as it was in Argentina, is necessary for the state to institutionalize the legal and organizational capacity to enforce the principle of equal responsibility in the face of the law.[25] And this principle is a constitutive feature of any democratic system.

The issue of responsibility for the past is broader in scope in Eastern Europe and may have more profound consequences: to the extent to which communist parties were coextensive with state administrations, decommunization entails extensive purges in the bureaucratic and to some extent in the industrial management sectors. Moreover, faced with the continuing economic crisis, democratic politicians in Eastern Europe tend to assign the responsibility for the economic crisis either to the remnants of the communist nomenklatura within the bureaucracy or to former communists who converted, to use Tarkowski's (1989) phrase, from apparatchiks to "entrepreneurtchiks." Hence, the slogan of purifying the state and the economy is popular, and several countries have passed or are about to pass legislation restricting the political rights of variously defined categories of former communist government or party officials. This purification deprives individuals of political rights on a collective basis and without due process, as well as depriving the state of a large number of potentially loyal and competent members of the state bureaucracies.

In sum, many new democracies face simultaneously multiple challenges of providing an effective citizenship under economic and institutional conditions that undermine the viability of state institutions. The result is that states are incapable of uniformly enforcing standardized bundles of rights and obligations that constitute citizenship. We thus face democratic political regimes without effective citizenship in large geographic areas or for significant social sectors. And without effective citizenship, it is doubtful whether such regimes constitute "democracies" in any meaningful sense of the term.

3. Democratic Institutions

Democracies are not all the same. Systems of representation, arrangements for the division and supervision of powers, manners of organization of interests, legal doctrines, and bundles of rights and obligations associated with citizenship differ significantly across regimes that are generally recognized as democratic.

All societies facing the task of constructing democracy face three generic issues: substance versus procedure, agreement versus competition, and majoritarianism versus constitutionalism. Should democratic institutions be expressly organized to facilitate reaching some normative objectives – typically conceptualized a social justice or a commitment to some set of values such as Christianity – or should they be neutral with regard to all values – promoting only liberty and political equality, establishing only procedures, and leaving substantive outcomes to the democratic process? Should democratic institutions be imbued with a moral content or should they be just a system of laws regulating conflicts? Which decisions should be made by agreement and which by competition? Must some institutions, such as constitutional tribunals, the armed forces, or monarchs, stand as arbiters above the competitive process, or should they all be subject to periodic verdicts of elections? Should some decisions, such as the right to private property in the Venezuelan and the Spanish constitutions or the separation between the church and the state, be removed from the competitive realm? Finally, to what extent and by what means should society bind itself to prevent some future transformations? Should the outcomes of the democratic process be sensitive to the will of current majorities, or should institutions restrain this will by constitutional provisions?[26]

A central distinctive task of democratic institutions is to counteract increasing returns to power. As Lane (1979) emphasized, power is a natural monopoly, since it exhibits increasing returns to scale: directly, to the extent that incumbency gives advantage, and indirectly, to the extent that political power can be used to acquire economic power and economic power can be used to gain political power. Hence, if democracy is not to evolve into a de facto dictatorship, democratic institutions must furnish the losers with instruments to counteract these effects. They must, in other words, protect the power of the minorities. If they do not, democracy will not be stabilized, since those who have lost in the first rounds of democratic competition will have good reasons to fear that they would never have a fair chance. Yet the issue of whether democratic institutions should provide only procedural guarantees, leaving the substantive outcomes open-ended, or whether they should be imbued with a moral or a social content remains central to contemporary controversies.

One way to pose this issue is to define it as the relation between political and social democracy: must some social or economic conditions be present if democracy is to exist in the political realm? We must be careful, however, to distinguish the normative from the empirical aspect of this question. From the normative point of view, one may argue that unless some social and economic conditions are in fact present in a given society, we would not want to consider it democratic even if elections occur regularly and peacefully. Indeed, there is extensive evidence that for most people ''democracy'' means first and foremost equality, in the social and economic as well as political realms. Yet this is not the same as to hypothesize that unless these conditions are present, democracy in this minimalist sense must wither away. The normative and the empirical aspects of this relation between democracy in the political and social realms are examined next but they must be kept carefully apart.

We have seen that even without leaving the purely political conception of democracy, one is led to a concern with social conditions as a prerequisite for an effective exercise of citizenship. Yet traditionally, as it developed in Western Europe, democracy was subject to a further-reaching claim, namely, that democratic institutions should generate outcomes that protect not only the liberties of citizens but also their material well-being. And this is what most people expect of new democracies. Survey data for Chile indicate that 64 percent of respondents expected democracy to reduce unemployment and 59 percent to attenuate social inequalities (Alaminos 1991). Surveys conducted by Bruszt and Simon (1991) in nine Eastern European countries show that people associate social and economic transformations with the advent of democracy. The proportion of respondents associating a major or some improvement of economic conditions ranged from 72 percent in the former Czechoslovakia and Slovenia to 96 percent in Romania. The proportion associating greater social equality ranged from 61 percent in Czechoslovakia to 88 percent in Bulgaria. The proportion associating many or some more jobs and less unemployment varied from 48 percent in Czechoslovakia to 92 percent in Romania.

Yet, whether one accepts the narrow or the broad version of this normative claim, the contentious question is whether it is best accomplished under a system of institutions limited to procedures or a system guaranteeing social rights. The traditional argument in favor of procedural democracy is that if democratic institutions are to last, they must constitute a framework that is open-ended, capable of processing divergent as well as changing interests and values. In this view, democratic institutions survive only if organized political forces, whatever their values may be, repeatedly find it in their interest to channel their actions within the democratic framework. The assumption that underlies this argument is that individuals are guided only by the prospects of advancing their interests and values rather than by a prior normative commitment to democracy. Yet Przeworski (1991) has shown that this view implies not only that democratic institutions must be "fair," in the sense of providing all major political forces a reasonable chance to advance their objectives within the institutional framework, but also that they must protect the interests of those forces that repeatedly lose in the democratic competition. Hence, the liberal hypothesis is true only if the liberal institutions are so designed as to provide fair access and protect the losers.[27]

The major argument in favor of substantive conceptions of democracy is that if we accept that democracy should lead to the development of social rights, the institutional framework should expressly facilitate or even guarantee the exercise of such rights.[28] In this view, democratic institutions must express values and guide moral choices rather than simply process whatever these might happen to be. Democratic institutions that fail to provide moral leadership cannot cope with conflicts originating from economic inequality and deprivation. Constitutional commitments act not only to guarantee but also to mobilize: without their institutional recognition, there are no rights to defend. Consent to democracy is contingent in this view not on the specific outcomes of the democratic process, but on the congruence between the moral content of institutions and the basic values of a society. Yet the counterargument is that this moral content will not be implemented anyway if political forces pursue their particularistic interests in the democratic competition. The danger is that moral commitments will remain hortatory, without microfoundations, and that such democratic constitutions will fail to regulate conflicts.

Thus, these normative considerations do not point to a clear choice. On the one hand, to acquire legitimacy, the framework of basic political institutions must reflect intensely felt normative commitments and shared goals. On the other hand, if a constitution stipulates social and economic rights that cannot be implemented given the fiscal situation or the organizational weak-

ness of the state, the institutional system will suffer from birth by its inca-
pacity to make effective the rights it guarantees.

Even if we had clear normative grounds for balancing substance and procedure, agreement and competition, majoritarianism and constitutionalism,
the emergent effects of specific institutional arrangements are far from clear.
Hence, it is perhaps safer to seek hypotheses at a lower level of abstraction,
by inquiring what we know about the consequences of specific institutional
arrangements under particular historical conditions: which institutions make
democracies work and last under what conditions?

Institutions have two distinct effects: (1) Although systematic evidence is
limited, there are sufficient grounds to believe that the specific institutional
arrangements that make a particular system democratic affect its performance.
Democracies are not all the same, and what they are matters for how they
perform. (2) In turn, the effect of exogenous circumstances on the survival
of democracies depends on the particular institutional arrangements. Democratic stability is not just a matter of economic, social, or cultural conditions
because specific institutional arrangements differ in their ability to process
conflicts, particularly when these conditions become so adverse that democratic performance is experienced as inadequate.

What then do we know about the effects of particular institutional arrangements for the performance and durability of democracy? In general, the institutional features that political scientists consider important are whether the
executive is responsible to the legislature, whether the electoral system is
proportional, whether the legislature is uni- or bicameral, whether legislative
committees are numerous and important, whether the system is unitary or
federal, whether there are important constitutional restrictions on majority
rule (including judicial review), whether central banks are independent of
governments, and whether membership in interest associations is voluntary
or compulsory. Powell (1990) lists as most important the following features
of democratic institutions: (1) degree of inclusiveness: what part of the membership must agree before a policy is accepted with regard to ordinary legislation and the constitution itself; (2) majoritarianism versus constitutionalism; (3) presidentialism, parliamentarism, and mixed systems; (4) election
rules. In another work (1989), he also emphasizes (5) the strength of legislative committees. A slightly different list is offered by Lijphart's (1989)
extension of his "consociational" to "consensus" democracy and by Weaver
and Rockman (1993) in their conclusion of a book entitled *Do Institutions Matter?*

The institutions the effects of which have been examined quite extensively are presidentialism versus parliamentarism, electoral systems, central banks, and collective bargaining systems. We also have some empirical studies of the consequences of investiture rules, majority- versus minority-favoring institutions, and legislative committee structures (Strom 1990, Powell 1991).

Ever since Rae's (1967) classical study, we know that electoral electoral formulae, district size, registration procedures, and compulsory voting have consequences for the structure of the party systems and for voter turnout (Blais and Carty 1988, 1990; Jackman 1987; King 1989, 1990; King and Browning 1987; Lijphart 1990, 1991; Powell 1982, 1989, 1990; Strom 1990). These in turn have an impact on the formation of majority governments and their durability. We know that investiture rules also help determine whether governments are majoritarian and whether they last. Investiture rules affect cabinet composition (Strom 1985) and duration (King et al. 1990). They favor or discriminate against smaller parties (Budge, Laver, and Strom 1994).

In turn, majority-favoring institutions clarify the responsibility for the policy outcomes and enable voters to punish the parties they hold responsible for bad performance (Powell 1989). Hence, such institutions may create incentives for governments to behave in a manner responsive to the views of majorities. Yet, as Shugart and Carey (1992: 7–8) pointed out, there is a trade-off between what they call "efficiency" – "the ability of elections to serve as a means for voters to identify and choose among the competing government options" – and "representativeness," defined as "the ability of elections to articulate and provide voice in the *assembly* for diverse interests." Shugart and Carey go on to argue that one particular system of institutions – "premier-presidentialism" – is the best compromise between the two.

The effects of the independence of central banks on economic performance are not easy to establish, in part because effective independence (as proxied by turnover rate of bank managers) does not always correspond to legal provisions (Cukierman, Webb, and Neyapti 1992). Among the developed countries, the independence of central banks tends to reduce inflation and increase unemployment without a clear effect on growth, but among the less developed countries the effect on inflation does not show in statistical analyses (Alesina 1988; Cukierman et al. 1992; Grilli, Masciandrano, and Tabellini 1991; Parkin 1986).

Finally, studies of the developed capitalist societies tend to show that until the early 1980s better economic performance was enjoyed by countries in which encompassing, centralized unions concerted with employers in the presence of the state controlled by social democratic parties.[29] Statistical analyses of the OECD countries show repeatedly, although not invariably, that lower income inequality, more extensive welfare services, and more favorable trade-off between employment and inflation, on the one hand, between wage rates and investment, on the other hand, are to be found in those countries that combined strong unions with social democratic control over the government. Moreover, the research of Lee and Przeworski (1993) concerning fourteen OECD countries between 1960 and 1981 shows that the welfare – defined as the utility, taking into account risk aversion, of a lottery composed of market income, unemployment compensation, and social wage – of an average adult was higher in the social democratic countries. To put it simply, the only countries in the world where almost no one is poor after taxes and transfers are the countries that pursued social democratic policies.[30]

Conversely, we have some evidence that the impact of economic crises on the survival of democracy depends on the institutional framework. Zimmerman (1987, 1988) pointed out that the depth and the timing of the recession of 1929–1932 does not predict whether democracy survived this crisis. Several students of the Brazilian crisis of 1961–1964 attributed the collapse of democracy not to the economic crisis but to the "institutional paralysis." What seemed to matter in these cases was whether the institutional framework was capable of generating effective majorities.

There are controversies about whether presidential or parliamentary democracies are more vulnerable to breakdown. Stepan and Skach (1992), as well as Mainwaring (1992) and Alvarez and Przeworski (1994), found that presidential systems are more likely to collapse. Linz (1994), in turn, argued that while presidential and parliamentary regimes may be equally vulnerable, there is considerable evidence that the presidential system contributed much to a number of those breakdowns. Yet these results are contested by Shugart and Carey (1992), who introduce finer distinctions among the presidential systems.

One finding that appears to be clear is that democracies do not survive when they combine presidentialism with a fractionalized party system (Stepan and Skach 1992, Alvarez and Przeworski 1994). And they often do combine: according to Stepan and Skach, among thirty-eight non-OECD countries between 1973 and 1989 presidential systems were accompanied by legislative majorities in 48 percent of cases, while parliamentary systems had majorities in 83 percent of cases. Yet only one among the twenty-five most recent democracies chose a pure parliamentary system, and almost all chose electoral systems with a fair dose of proportionality. In several presidential or semipresidential systems, the main line of political conflict, particularly about the economic reform strategy, is between the president and the congress, rather than among political parties. Peru, Nicaragua, and Russia, where conflicts between the president and the congress led to the closing of legislatures, are but extreme cases of what is occurring in Brazil and in Poland. One mechanism that makes pure presidential and mixed systems fragile is that such systems often generate conflicts that either have no clear resolution in the absence of arbitrating powers or lead to a legislative stalemate. The Bolivian Congress once "broke relations" with the president; the Nicaraguan Congress split in 1992 into anti- and pro-presidential bodies. Situations in which the executive does not have sufficient support in the congress to pass legislation but does have sufficient strength to have his or her vetoes sustained are endemic in presidential systems, and they lead at times to a complete paralysis: in some countries (Brazil between 1961 and 1964, Chile between 1970 and 1973), not a single piece of ordinary legislation is passed.

While the empirical knowledge of institutional effects is rapidly accumulating, the present state of knowledge is not yet sufficient to foresee which specific institutional arrangements work and last under various historical conditions. Should Poland adopt a parliamentary or a presidential system, a proportional representation or a majority-favoring electoral system, a uni- or bicameral legislature? Since most empirical studies are limited to the OECD countries and most consider institutional features one at a time, we do not yet know enough to make such recommendations. It is noteworthy that an article, by an authoritative source, entitled "Choosing a Constitution in East Europe: Lessons from Public Choice," is completely ad hoc when it comes to political recommendations (Mueller 1991). In turn, the idea that all countries should simply imitate the genius of the U.S. Constitution (Robinson 1991) is a recipe for disaster.

A separate institutional problem concerns civil–military relations. With the exception of Poland, no southern or East European transition began from the base of a hierarchically led military government. The regime in Greece was led nonhierarchically by colonels, and this helps explain why generals, in the interest of reestablishing the institutional hierarchy, supported the democratic government's imprisonment of the colonels. In sharp contrast, hierarchically led military regimes were the norm in Latin America. And unless such a military organization is defeated or disbanded by a domestic, revolutionary, or external armed force, it will withdraw after the transition into the state apparatus, where it normally has substantial prerogatives and organizational resources.

This strategic position of the military has already had a major impact on transitional politics in Latin America. In some cases, such as Guatemala, military prerogatives remain so extensive that elected civilian governments never, in fact, become democracies. In other cases, such as Brazil and Uruguay, the founding elections were strongly structured by the military. In Chile, the military control of the state, and its insistence on the maintenance of their authoritarian 1980 constitution as the price of transition, will probably put off a complete democratic transition until the end of the 1990s. Nicaragua is close to being a civil–military dierarchy. In Peru, both Fernando Belaunde Terry and Alan Garcia, the first two elected presidents, abdicated all responsibility for the exercise of state force to the military. The "delegative democracy" of Alberto Fujimori rapidly disintegrated into a military-backed dictatorship. Latin America's second-oldest continuous democracy, Venezuela, was severely shaken by military uprisings in which the combination of severe stabilization policies and flamboyant corruption contributed to a climate where military rebels were backed by substantial civilian praise and organized demonstration.

Civil–military relations in the communist states differed from those in the capitalist peripheries. The armed forces were subordinated to the communist parties and integrated within the state system in which the party was the principal force. They were able, however, to retain a high degree of internal autonomy, functioning as states within states. They were also frequently represented in the highest executive organs (political bureaus). With the exception of Poland (and in this case only after 1981), they never dominated the political system. During the transition from communism, the armed forces posture ranged from active support (Poland, Romania) to neutrality. In none of the communist states did the armed forces intervene to prevent the transition. Yet the very fact that, in general, they are not being blamed for the vices of the communist regimes increases the likelihood that the military could be induced to intervene if the new democracies encounter serious internal difficulties. Polish opinion data show a lasting pattern of public confidence in the military, which gradually surpassed all the representative institutions and organizations, and even the church. Moreover, the likelihood of a military intervention is magnified by (1) the fact that the economic crisis results in the collapse of state budgets, including military expenditures, (2) the evaporation of a sense of mission, resulting from the change of the geopolitical situation, and (3) the tendency of postcommunist governments to purge the armed forces of high-ranking officers from the old regime, which creates a feeling of insecurity among the officer corps.

There are, of course, some favorable conditions concerning the role of the military. The ideologies that rationalized the military rule in the past, whether internal subversion or nationalist developmentalism, lost their credibility. Although the ouster of democratically elected governments in Pakistan and Thailand caused little world reaction, the international political climate is strongly adverse to military regimes. In many countries, especially in Uruguay and Argentina, the military is no longer considered a reliable ally by dominant classes.

What does this picture of civil–military relations imply for sustaining democracy? Three dimensions are particularly important. First, democratic leaders must have a policy of constitutional control, where they integrate military and strategic policies into the overall policy of the government. To date, no country in Latin America has devised a consistent policy of military reform as was accomplished in Spain. Second, the reform of democratic political institutions themselves should be on the agenda. Finally, power is always relational, and if state capacity is eroded, and if important social sectors continue to bear disproportionately the costs of economic restructuring, this may create the conditions in which the military, in comparative terms, gains in organizational, ideological, and political power.

As we have thus far seen, there are reasons to think that specific institutional arrangements do matter for the durability and performance of democracies. How then are these institutional arrangements selected when democratic regimes are being constructed? Specifically, can we expect that conflicting political forces will settle on the institutional framework that is most conducive to sustain democracy?

Contrary to the hypothesis of O'Donnell and Schmitter (1986), which guided the initial studies of democratization, there is little evidence that the features of post-transition systems correspond either to the traits of the ancien régime or to modalities of transition. The mode of transition may set up an "elective affinity" for specific institutional systems, but this proclivity can be deflected by (1) the strength of a particular national constitutional heritage (presidentialism in Latin America, proportional representation in Europe), (2) the conjunctural saliency of some specific pattern of cleavage or international threat (Czech presidentialism); and (3) the existence of powerful foreign models and sponsors (the 5 percent exclusion clause, the mixed electoral system, the vote of constructive no confidence: all items in the German Federal constitution). It is true that transitions to democracy often leave institutional traces, in particular when they subject democracy to the tutelage of an autonomous military. But these traces can be gradually wiped away: in Spain, the successive democratic governments were effective in removing the remnants of Francismo and in placing the military under civilian control; in Poland, the evolving relations of forces eliminated most of the relics of the Magdalenka pact.

The political forces involved in establishing the new democratic system may initially share a minimal common conception of what democracy is (or perhaps of what it is not), but as they attempt to establish definite rules and institutions they discover that they differ on what these should be. Even if everyone knew the consequences of particular institutional arrangements, institutional issues would still generate conflicts because institutions have distributional consequences (Knight 1992). If the choice of institutions were just a matter of efficiency, disagreements would be just a matter of divergent views as to the best way of reaching it: no one would have reason to fear a system that makes someone better off at no cost to anyone else. But, given the distribution of resources, institutions do affect the manner and the degree in which particular interests and values can be advanced. Hence, preferences concerning institutions differ. Given the constituencies they claim to represent – whether class, region, religion, ethnicity, or language – particular political forces prefer different institutional arrangements, and they enter into often protracted conflicts about the institutional framework.

Conflicts over institutions are likely to be protracted. The actors bargaining over the institutions are unlikely to "get it right" the first time: it often takes several attempts before a stable framework emerges. While transitions to democracy entail by definition a transformation of the institutional system, in particular free elections, they do not necessarily cause changes in the relation of political forces, policy orientations, or the economic and social patterns. Hence, those who expected that the transition to democracy would lead not only to a political but also a social revolution are disappointed. The issue of *continuismo* appears on the political agenda in most new democracies, typically as an argument that any continuity constitutes prima facie evidence that transition did not take place or at least that it was "incomplete." Yet while some of those continuities are due to the negotiated character of the transition, most persist simply because the change of the political regime is not sufficient to transform social and economic relations. As Choi (1991) shows, South Korea is an extreme case, since in that country the authoritarian establishment was able for some time to organize as an electoral party, win elections, and continue using almost the same mechanisms of clientelism and repression as before. Taiwan may soon follow this pattern. This form of continuity differs from those cases where control over the government offices changed hands but the military continued to exercise a tutelage over the competitive system, as in Chile; it also differs from those cases where the continuity remains within the bureaucracy and yet is distinct from the countries where it resides mainly in the control over economic resources, say, the Philippines. Nevertheless, the issue of whether the transition to democracy has been completed tends to generate endless debates among the political actors involved as well as among scholarly observers.

The most obvious and comprehensive moment when an effort is made to choose a type of democracy usually involves the drafting and ratifying of a new constitution. Not only do such documents lay out an explicit matrix of institutions and a formal distribution of their competencies, but they do so by means of general norms that are supposed to govern behavior (and establish legitimacy) in a wide range of private and public transactions.

Two general features of constitutionalism are particularly relevant. First, it seeks to define the future substance as well as the form of politics by placing certain political, and at times also social and economic, rights beyond the reach of democratic uncertainty. Constitutions assure powerful minorities that their vital interests will not be violated by transitory shifts of the power relations. Second, to make such assurances credible, constitutions bind not just their drafters but future generations. Hence, they resound with eternal ("self-evident") principles, they are difficult to amend, and they empower specific institutions (a supreme court, a council of state) with an independent capacity to monitor their application.

An important question, therefore, is, How do various factors characterizing the situations under which the choice of institutions occurs affect the constitutional outcomes? Unfortunately, we have little systematic empirical knowledge to guide us. Ozbudun (1992) argued that the democratic or nondemocratic nature of constitution making, its timing, and style play an important role in determining the stability of the constitutions. The crucial distinction is between those constitutions that result from a process of extensive compromise and widespread acceptance and those that are enacted by a victorious majority over the objections of minorities. With regard to democratic or less than fully democratic constitution-making procedures (the latter includes constitution making by a nonelected or partially elected assembly, or by a reasonably freely elected assembly dominated by the incumbents of the former authoritarian regime, or by a freely elected assembly that has to operate under strong de facto constraints), there is some evidence that democratic constitution-making procedures are generally associated with stable, and nondemocratic procedures with unstable constitutions. Consensual constitutions would seem to have more of the intended freezing effect on subsequent content and behavior. But even dissatisfied minorities may discover that they can live under dissensual constitutions provided that the basic rule of contingent consent is respected, in other words, that they can compete fairly for majority support and can confidently expect to form future governments if successful. Moreover, they are likely to learn that modern constitutions (despite their increasing length and detail) cannot cover all eventualities. Lacunae and ambiguities will provide opportunities for developing extraconstitutional arrangements and engaging in unconventional behaviors. The "flexible interpretation" of specific constitutional norms may permit the democratic process to adopt new forms and alter old ones, especially in those polities that have not yet established an independent judiciary.

With regard to timing, Przeworski (1991: chap. 2) conjectured that institutions chosen early in the process of transition, before the relations of force among the conflicting parties are clarified, are more likely to protect the eventual losers and are therefore more likely to be stable in the face of changing conditions. Yet constitutions adopted early may tend to be excessively antiauthoritarian, in the sense that they focus on protecting rights at the cost of enabling governance. In this view, constitutions adopted after some period of turmoil are more likely to strike an appropriate balance between the protection of individual and minority rights and the authorization of effective governance.

While we offer conflicting hypotheses, one conclusion that is apparent is that there are no grounds to expect that the institutional framework that emerges is the one most likely to work and last under the given historical conditions. Institutions are established as a result of conflicts among partisan forces, and as in many strategic situations, the pursuit of partisan rationality is likely to generate collectively suboptimal outcomes.

Moreover, while constitutions are the single most important organizing principle of democracies, we should warn against overestimating the importance of constitutional choice. Constitutions appear to offer a solution to conflicts that emerge in new democracies by virtue of the belief that giving a particular form to the resolution of political conflicts will per se modify the substance of political demands and alter the strategies of political actors. Yet while such formalisms are not without their independent significance, it would be hazardous to center attention exclusively on the legal framework delimiting the powers of institutions and the rights of citizens as the hallmark of democratic consolidation. Constitutions need not be "periodical literature," but neither are they holy writ. Modern democracies are bound to be constitutional, but the processes of selection, access, participation, competition, accountability, and responsiveness are simply too multiple and mutable to be definitively codified.

Thus, while institutions have an autonomous impact on the performance and durability of democracies, their effects depend on the political and cultural context in which they function. And one cannot assume that all the political and cultural conditions that characterize the countries in which democracy was established decades ago are present in the countries that have only recently experienced transitions to democracy, often for the first time ever or at least after a long authoritarian hiatus. We must ask, therefore, what kinds of democratic institutions are compatible with the conditions most likely to be found in the new democracies?

4. Civil Society

Preliminary research, as well as personal observations, seem to indicate that the new democracies lack several conditions which are assumed in the light of the experience of earlier democracies to be necessary for the stability of democratic institutions based on universal suffrage. When one puts together piecemeal observations, one arrives at a list of such "absences" that is almost comprehensive: no effective parties (Di Tella 1991), no encompassing unions and other representative institutions, no national bourgeoisies capable of offering a hegemonic project ("capitalism without capitalists," Rychard 1991, also Domański et al. 1993), no stable political class (Weffort 1991), no clearly identifiable political forces (Bruszt 1989, Rychard 1991), even no crystallized structure of interests to be represented (Bruszt and Simon 1991, Kolarska-Bobińska 1991). Not only the state but also the civil society is weak in most new democracies.[31]

In the historical development of Western Europe, political parties, along with labor unions, were the main mechanism of incorporation of the masses into the political system. Indeed, recent research shows (Rueschemeyer, Stephens, and Stephens 1992) that working-class parties were the main force in bringing democracy. By organizing class and other interests, they became instruments by which those groups that suffered from poverty and oppression by virtue of their place in the economic system could struggle for the improvement of their material and cultural conditions. At the same time, by channeling the pursuit of interests and values into the institutional framework of competitive politics, political parties regularized intergroup conflicts. While democratic institutions create the possibility for conflicts to be processed in a rule-governed and limited manner, political parties, particularly those of the Left, disciplined the economically and culturally disadvantaged masses to pursue their interests within those institutions.

For reasons that need not detain us here (Di Tella 1991), with the notable exception of Chile, similar parties did not historically develop in Latin American countries, where the dominant sectors never overcame the fear of the political mobilization of the lower classes and where, in turn, this mobilization often assumed the form of movements rather than electoral parties. In particular, populist movements were the widespread form of political organization of the underprivileged in Latin America, especially but not exclusively in countries at intermediate levels of development. In their typical form, such movements organized the masses experiencing early stages of urban and industrial life under the leadership of nonrevolutionary elites drawn from the upper and middle strata. They have produced popular mobilization and brought about redistributions of income but showed little capacity to create solid institutional structures.

Political parties experience today a continuing decline almost everywhere. And they are fragmented, organizationally weak, and unrepresentative in most new democracies. One reason for this weakness may be generic. The birth of democracy creates a dilemma for the proper role of the opposition: how much to oppose and by what means. If the opposition does oppose vigorously, democracy may be threatened. Particularly under difficult economic conditions, intransigent opposition may create an ungovernable situation. Hence, vigorous competition, and clear party differentiation, appears dangerous when representative institutions are still fragile. As a result, political forces often seek to establish a ''pact,'' an agreement to distribute offices and to pursue particular policies. Such pacts may be necessary not only to reduce the level of political conflict but also to create incentives for political leaders to remain within the limits of democracy (Schmitter 1984). It is worth noting that in several cases of democratization, the party that won the first election used its control over the state to establish itself as a clientelistic machine that continued for decades to control office: this was the case in Italy, Japan, and India. In some other countries, notably Venezuela and Colombia, parties created a duopoly that divided the spoils and shared influence over policies.

Yet pacts are exclusionary: they constitute cartels of incumbents against contenders, cartels that restrict competition, bar access, and distribute benefits of political power among the insiders. They thus create the danger that democracy would turn into a private project of leaders of some political parties and corporatist associations who extract private benefits and protect their rents by excluding outsiders. Moreover, if the opposition does not oppose, does not present alternatives, and does not struggle energetically for these alternatives, the representative power of political institutions, their capacity to mobilize and to incorporate, is weak. Democracy becomes anemic.

As we have noted earlier, electoral systems do shape party structures. The adoption of unlimited proportional representation or highly complex multiple electoral systems in several Eastern European countries facilitates the fragmentation and the instability of the party system. Before the elections of

1993, Poland had the highest degree of party fragmentation ever recorded (Stepan and Skatch 1992). As a result, politicians spent most of their time on efforts to build a coalition that could govern: the four largest parties were not sufficient to form a majority in the parliament. Membership in political parties is negligible in all Eastern European countries, and electoral turnout is low by all comparative standards.

A strong control by parties of the lists of parliamentary candidates, in which the voter chooses not the candidate but the party (as in a system of closed and blocked lists), may be thus convenient at the early stage of democracy. Yet as new democracies become consolidated, such control may lead to a domination of politics by bureaucratic oligarchies, more concerned about the machinery of their parties than about their voters and constituencies. This became an important issue in Greek and Spanish politics several years after democracy was reestablished. Recent survey data in Spain reveal a strong criticism of the system of closed and blocked lists, which are seen as contributing to popular disaffection with politicians (Demoscopia, 1992).

Internal party democracy also affects popular views on politics. Yet there is no clear formula for an adequate combination of internal party pluralism and unity: internecine struggles are not only a good recipe for electoral defeats, but also a possible cause of regime instability; yet internal authoritarianism and oligarchical politics increase the distance between society and political institutions.

Systems of interest representation are rarely chosen in the same fashion as are systems of electoral representation or of executive power. For one, the relation between formal legal rules and institutional outcomes is much less determinate since many of the practices of trade unions, business and professional associations, social movements, and public-interest groups emerge from informal interactions within civil society. They are only loosely and indirectly affected by the provisions of the civil and criminal codes, antitrust legislation (if it exists), the tax system, and so forth. For another, the constitutions of virtually all new democracies proclaim "freedom of association," "freedom of assembly," and "freedom of petition," but the effective use of these rights depends on a complex calculus by individuals and collectivities that can be facilitated but rarely ensured by formal rules and government incentives. Like most rights that are equally available, those concerning interest representation are very unequally exercised.

Moreover, unlike electoral representation and executive power, where it is usually easy to distinguish between the roles and their occupants before and after regime change, functional representation normally preserves a good deal more continuity with the ancien régime. Authoritarian regimes typically follow policies of "state corporatism" and deliberately sponsor the formation of a set of officially recognized, monopolistic interest representatives. Democracies have a difficult time breaking with these practices and disposing of their organizational and material legacies. A sudden shift to a purely voluntaristic and free format could jeopardize the very existence of some organized interests, many of which played an active role in the emancipation process, and could produce a very skewed pattern of representation.

The underlying tendency, however, is clear: democratization encourages pluralism, that is, a system composed of a multiplicity of overlapping, competing organizations that act autonomously of each other and the state in determining the categories they claim to represent and the tactics they use to advance their interests.

Democratization would also seem to shift the balance of competing forces toward those interest categories – labor, consumers, renters, women – that are composed of large numbers of relatively dispersed and subordinate actors and that have frequently been oppressed by authoritarian rulers. Ironically, however, under the new conditions of voluntary associability and multiple channels of representation, these pluralistically organized interests tend to decline and lose influence relative to those representing smaller, more compact, and privileged groups.

Yet trade unions experience difficulties similar to those of political parties. They are numerically weak in new democracies: Grassi (1992) found that Argentina, at about 30 percent, had the highest rate of unionization among the fourteen non-Eastern European recent cases of transition to democracy. In Eastern Europe and the former Soviet Union, only Poland and Bulgaria have numerically significant union movements.

Politically, these are not propitious times for trade unions. On the one hand, they are identified by the neoliberal ideology as one of the main culprits for economic "rigidity," a "special interest" threatening economic efficiency. On the other hand, trade unions face a dilemma when confronted with the intertemporal trade-offs inherent in market-oriented reforms: accepting these trade-offs is a highly demobilizing strategy with regard to the rank and file; rejecting them appears to be, and often is, irresponsible. Moreover, in many countries, particularly South Korea, the transition to democracy in the electoral realm did not reduce the traditional authoritarian pattern of repression with regard to labor organizing. One should not forget that the growth of labor organizations was a long and bloody process in the West, where for decades the very existence of unions was seen, on the Right and the Left, as signifying the end of capitalism.

Thus, both political parties and trade unions find it difficult to organize and represent, for reasons that can be attributed to institutional factors, as well as general political and economic conditions. But we have a gnawing intuition – no more than intuition – that something more profound is involved. It is the absence of collective projects, of socially integrating ideologies, of clearly identifiable political forces, of crystallized structures of interests to be represented. Sociologists in several countries, old democracies and new, are discovering that correlations among different political attitudes as well as between political attitudes and partisan preferences have declined.

The reasons for this weak structuration of interests are not apparent. One may be that many new democracies, particularly those in Eastern Europe, are undergoing a major transformation of property relations. When property relations are in flux, people do not know for sure where their interests lie and identities are confused. No class-based interests can emerge. In this view, "in all Eastern European societies the base for the pattern of socialization typical of civil society would emerge only after the dissolution of state ownership" (Staniszkis 1992: 222). Yet the fact that a similar pattern can be observed in the established democracies places such explanations in doubt. Perhaps what we are observing is not "individualism" nor "anomie" but just a tacit agreement that collective choices are so constrained by to a large extent international, economic, and political factors that little is at stake in political participation. Since politicians do not offer alternatives, people do not perceive them.

Survey data indicate that new democracies often show a syndrome consisting of the mistrust of politics and politicians, sentiments of personal political inefficacy, low confidence in democratic institutions, and dissatisfaction with the performance of the actual democratic institutions. Yet curiously, the belief in democracy as the best form of government does not bear an obvious relation to these attitudes.

In southern Europe, ten years after democracy had been reestablished, about half of the citizens of Spain and Portugal expressed indifference, boredom, and mistrust toward politics; only one out of every four survey respondents fitted the ideal of an interested and participative citizen (Montero and Torcal 1990). The satisfaction with the actual performance of democracy varied substantially among the three southern European countries: fifteen years after democracy had been reestablished, 63 percent of Greek citizens declared that they were not satisfied with the state of democracy in their country, a degree of dissatisfaction 20 percentage points above the average of the European Union. In Portugal and Spain, however, dissatisfaction was much less frequent. The actual political and economic performance of the new democracies seems to have mattered: whereas in Greece dissatisfaction increased by twenty points between 1985 and 1990, a period of considerable economic difficulties, dissatisfaction declined by the same proportion in Portugal, where this period was marked by economic expansion and political stability (*Eurobarometer*, October–November 1985 and June 1990). Yet at the same time, support for democracy as an ideal remained high in all three countries, apparently unrelated to specific conditions. Thus, in the middle of the economic adjustment of the 1980s, 87 percent of Greeks, 70 percent of Spaniards, and 61 percent of Portuguese declared their unconditional support for democracy. Those who accepted dictatorship under certain circumstances were always a small minority, which oscillated in the three countries between 5 and 10 percent; those who thought that for people like themselves the political regime did not matter represented between 6 and 9 percent of the population.

Latin American countries exhibit divergent patterns. At the end of the 1980s, 75 percent of Brazilians believed that politicians tried to enrich themselves with public money and to improve the material conditions of their friends and their families (Moisés 1990). Only 38 percent of Brazilians expressed confidence in the Congress and only 41 percent in the presidency, But contrary to the southern European pattern, in Brazil this disaffection toward political institutions and politicians did influence attitudes toward democracy as such. In 1991, the proportion of "unconditional democrats" in Brazil, 39 percent, was about half of that in southern Europe, while as many as 45 percent of Brazilians declared either that the political regime did not matter for people like themselves (28 percent) or that dictatorship would be preferable under some circumstances (17 percent). Although a majority accepted that democracy was better for political freedom, democratic regime was seen as worse than dictatorship in overall terms as well as in terms of economic performance and public morality (Lamounier 1992). Yet the legitimacy of democracy was much more extensive in Chile and Argentina, in spite of the poor economic performance of the latter. Thus, among the countries for which similar data are available, Brazil stands out as the society where the cultural foundations of consolidation seem to be eroded.

Citizens of the recent democracies of central and Eastern Europe also share the syndrome of disaffection with politics and politicians. Evidence for Hungary (Bruszt and Simon, 1991) shows that in 1990 nearly three out of every four citizens believed that politicians should never be trusted; only 40 percent declared to have confidence in parliament and in the government. In Poland, in early 1993, 49 percent of respondents thought most parliamentary deputies used their positions for personal gain and only 1 percent thought that no politician does so. Forty percent had confidence in the government and only 22 percent in either house of the parliament (CBOS, February 1993). Only one out of every twenty Poles and two out of every ten Hungarians considered that they could do something about an unfair decision taken by the government: this is a proportion three times lower than in the United Kingdom, but similar to Spain or Venezuela (Bruszt and Simon 1991). In 1990 dissatisfaction with the state of democracy in Bulgaria, Romania and Czechoslovakia was comparable with that in Greece. Yet in Hungary, the country where political and economic transitions have been relatively smooth, it extended to 85 percent of the population, while only slightly over a third thought that democracy could solve the problems of the country (Bruszt and Simon 1991). In mid-1993, only 1 percent of Poles thought that democracy was functioning well; 40 percent found the performance of democracy tolerable and 43 percent thought that it functioned so badly that if things continued, democracy would fall (CBOS, July 1993). The distribution of support for democracy in Poland is close to the Brazilian levels: while 62 percent of Poles see democracy as the superior form of government, 45 percent agree that there are some situations when nondemocratic government may be more desirable, and 44 percent agree that it makes no difference to them if the form of government is democratic.

Thus, in spite of skeptical attitudes toward politics and occasional dissatisfaction with the actual performance of democratic governments, the fact that even in the middle of the economic crisis of the early 1980s, democracy as such was questioned only by small minorities (Maravall 1981) indicates that a democratic commitment was consolidated in southern Europe. When the legitimacy of democracy becomes largely autonomous from its efficacy and when it is unconditionally accepted by large majorities, we have prima facie evidence of normative consolidation. Can we expect that a similar commitment to democracy will develop in the course of time in the other new democracies?

The generalized political mistrust, skepticism, and apathy in new democracies are certainly related to the prolonged experiences of dictatorship, a history of political turbulence and discontinuities, memories of manipulation, and a systematic transmission of values of depoliticization. It may thus be the case that the passing of time will reinforce the cultural roots of democracy and change perceptions of politics. The present weakness of organizational networks, which are hardly able to structure and channel the latent interests of diverse social groups and which contribute to feelings of powerlessness and to a lack of moral cohesion, may be thus gradually superseded. Also, expectations tend to explode in the initial stages of new democracies: the new regimes are expected to solve long-standing socioeconomic, administrative, and political problems. An optimistic conclusion, therefore, might be that after an inevitable phase of disenchantment, the link between legitimacy and performance would become gradually looser, until political institutions eventually enjoy, at least beyond some thresholds, a considerable degree of autonomy with regard to the particular outcomes.

Many of the assumptions underlying this optimistic view, however, are unwarranted. The passing of time, as the evolution of the Italian political culture shows, does not necessarily improve citizens' perceptions of democratic politics. Moreover, as the evidence for southern Europe shows, intermediate associations and social organizations – among them, trade unions – became weaker not stronger, at least in terms of affiliation, during the 1980s. Finally, nothing assures us that new democracies would generate early positive results in economic growth, social peace, or administrative efficiency. And there may be thresholds of performance below which the construction of democracy is affected. A complacent reliance on the passing of time ignores not just the political risks, but the fact that these subjective foundations of democracy are also affected by political decisions and policies.

The vast political changes that transitions to democracy bring about, the social and economic crises that often precede and accompany them, tend to have a deep impact on value systems. Traditional references disappear, ideologies are abandoned. Many transitions to democracy are rooted in material expectations. In turn, values of solidarity and fairness are often weak in new democracies. When the political cultures and the normative worlds of societies undergoing profound economic crises, sharp social inequalities, and extended poverty are penetrated by the values of individual success and speculative enrichment, the cultural roots of social cohesion are affected. The advice of Guizot, *enrichissez vous*, can hardly provide the moral fiber of democracy. The view of politics as abusive, the consideration that all politicians are the same, can be reinforced by the actual behavior of politicians. Democratic politics thus have moral and pedagogic components that cannot be neglected by politicians: political disaffection can be the result of this negligence, as well as of bad policies.

Democracy is also seriously challenged by several kinds of fundamentalist ideologies. Democratic institutions can last only if they are based on the ideological recognition that societies consist of groups with divergent values and interests, that conflicts of interests and values are natural in any complex society, and that these conflicts can be, always temporarily and reversibly, resolved only by recourse to procedures and institutions. The outcomes of the institutional process do not always appear as either rational or moral: persistent differences of opinion, passionate conflicts of interests, and procedural wranglings are often seen as threatening deeply held values. Democracy calls for a particular suspension of belief: the certainty that one outcome is best for all, rational or moral. Decisions by numbers or rules do not have prima facie rationality; consensus has a higher moral and cognitive status than outcomes originating just from following procedures. The everyday life of democratic politics is not a spectacle that inspires awe: an endless squabble among petty ambitions, rhetoric designed to hide and mislead, shady connections between power and money, laws that make no pretense to justice, policies that reinforce privilege. Hence, the perennial temptation to make everything transparent in one swoop, to replace politics with administration, anarchy with discipline, to do the moral or the rational – the authoritarian temptation.

This temptation is fueled by several ideologies. Nationalism provides one, religion another. Organicist views of the nation are incompatible with the toleration of partial interests. If the nation is an organism, it is not a body that can breed divisions and conflicts. Its unity is organic, that is, given by primordial ties that are presented as biological and eternal. In the words of the Polish nationalist ideologist Roman Dmowski (1989: 71), the nation is "a live social organism, having a spiritual specificity derived from racial and historical bases," not a body that can tolerate alien elements. Individualism and dissent are manifestations of not belonging. And, as O'Donnell (1991) has shown, the notion of an organic unity of interests leads each of the political forces to strive for a monopoly in representing "the" national interest. Political forces do not appear as parties representing partial interests against other partial values or projects. Each aspires to become the one and only representative of the nation, to cloak itself in the mantle of *el movimiento nacional*. Democracy is then just an interim moment of competition for the monopoly in representing the national interest.

Religious fundamentalism is incompatible with the tolerance of alternative value systems. Since democracy requires both respect for minorities' rights and a willingness to seek compromises, it can be seriously endangered by religious moral fanaticism, which, by definition, attempts to impose its rules on everyone and sees compromise as a betrayal of first principles. The rising wave of religious fundamentalism affects not only new democracies, but it can more easily be contained in those states that have well-established constitutional rules concerning the separation of church and state. In new democracies, there is often no institutional framework strong enough to deal with these issues and no cultural tradition to rely upon. While Islamic fundamentalism is the most evident example of such a challenge, some other regions are not immune to similar dangers. In the postcommunist countries, the intensity of religion has its origins in the historical ties between religion and ethnicity, as well as to the more recent conflict between communism and Christianity. The rising tide of religious fundamentalism is a reaction to past abuses of dictatorships that unsuccessfully tried to wipe out the influence of religious institutions and the popular attachment to religion. In the former Yugoslavia, religious fanaticism feeds conflicts between ethnic groups, in spite of their cultural closeness. In Poland, fundamentalist Catholic parties, with the explicit support of the Roman Catholic church, reject any notion of the separation between the state and the church and seek to impose their moral rules on the entire society. The Catholic church states openly that democracy must obey limits that are pregiven and that cannot be altered by the principle of popular sovereignty.

To sum up, there are indications that several conditions that are generally thought to sustain democratic institutions wherever they are well established are absent in the new democracies: representative organizations are weak, civil society is highly fragmented, memories of political abuse are still fresh, antidemocratic ideologies are quite alive. Clearly, we are not claiming that our list of the "absences" is equally comprehensive in all new democracies. Chile has political parties that represent effectively, Poland has encompassing trade unions, while the general ideal of democracy is widely accepted in most newly democratic countries. Yet, if we believe that many of these absences are specific to the new democracies, the question becomes whether democracy can survive under these conditions.

If we are to believe the immense body of literature following Lipset's (1960) seminal work (see Diamond 1992 for a recent review), the organizational, social, and cultural prerequisites of sustainable democracy are largely a matter of the level of economic development. Among the thirty-three democracies that have ever attained per capita income of $4,000, only in two cases was the democratic regime subverted: in Argentina in 1976 and in Uruguay in 1973. Among the 42 democracies that reached at least $3,000 of per capita income, authoritarian regimes followed in 8 cases: half of them in Argentina, in Chile in 1973, in Greece in 1967, in Turkey in 1979, and in Uruguay. Hence, the Argentine peculiarities aside, it seems true that, once established, democracies tend to somehow survive in the more economically developed countries. And most of the recently established democracies are above the threshold of at least $3,000: among the countries for which data are available, the most recent transition to democracy occurred at the highest level in Spain at $6,584, and at levels of $3,000 or more in Hungary at $5,530, Uruguay at $5,163, South Korea at $5,156, Greece at $4,521, Argentina at $4,180, Chile at $4,099 (1988 data), Poland at $4,083 (1987 data), Portugal at $3,813, Peru at $3,187 (1980 level declined since then to below $3,000), Turkey at $3,086, and Ecuador at $3,057 (1979 level declined since then to below $3,000). The poorest countries in which transitions occurred since 1980 are Honduras, which had an income of $1,300 in 1982, Bolivia (which has since declined) at $1,680 in 1982, and Philippines at $1,701 in 1986. And while democracy is much more brittle in poor countries, one should not forget that India has sustained regularly scheduled elections even though democracy was established when the country had a per capita income of $511 (1951 data), Sri Lanka has been a continuous democracy even though it had a per capita income of only $1,268 in 1951, and Japan although it had an income of only $1,580 in 1952 (Przeworski and Limongi 1993).

Yet, as persuasive as these numbers may be, the question remains, What kind of democracy is compatible with the absences we have diagnosed? A hypothesis has been offered by O'Donnell (1991), who examined a democratic regime from the point of view of the executive power. This power is related in stable democracies vertically to the public opinion via representative organizations and horizontally to other powers through the system of checks and balances. Some established democracies have weak representative systems (e.g., the U.S. Congress), some an executive which dominates other political institutions (e.g., the U.K.), but all of them have at least one of these linkages. Now in many new democracies there is little structuration of interests; political parties, unions, and other representative organizations are weak; and at the same time no functioning parliaments, autonomous judicial institutions, or supervisory organs exist. The executive becomes not a representative but a "delegate," suspended above the society composed of individuals and unchecked by other institutions. This proclivity to delegate is pronounced in the Bruszt–Simon (1991) surveys: the proportion of respondents who agree with the statement "As long as things are going on well, I am really not interested who is in power," ranged from 55 percent in former Czechoslovakia to 79 percent in Romania. Thus, the anecdote about a Brazilian voter who waited two hours in line to cast his vote in the last presidential election and, having acquitted himself of his citizenship responsibility, said, "Now I have done my share. The rest is theirs" is dangerously close to the story about the African ruler who announced, "I am the dictator people chose to put up with."

Anyone concerned with the quality of democracy will see such a political system as greatly impoverished. And the question of whether such democracies can last remains open. A central task of new democracies, we have argued, is to create the channels and the incentives for all the major political forces to process their interests within the framework of representative institutions. If decisions are made elsewhere, representative institutions wilt. They do not necessarily crumble: as O'Donnell has suggested, it is conceivable that such a system – what he calls "delegative democracy" – might be durable at least in the sense that regular elections can take place and civil rights can be observed even in systems in which the executive makes repeated recourse to decrees, checked from time to time only by public opinion polls or occasional riots. But, as we argue later, such a rule by decree is likely to be ineffective from the economic point of view: the reliance on decrees is a symptom of a weakness, not strength, of the state institutions vis-à-vis the civil society. Hence, this kind of a system is unattractive from the political point of view and ineffective from the economic point of view. The conditions in which, as Bruszt (1989; see also Kurczewska, Staszyńska, and Bojar 1993) put it, "a weak state confronts a weak civil society" do not augur well either for political or for economic effectiveness of democracy, particularly when democratic institutions face the challenge of transforming the economic system and overcoming an economic crisis.

Part II

MARKETS, PROPERTY SYSTEMS, AND ECONOMIC GROWTH

5. Economic Reforms in New Democracies

Criteria of Success of Market-Oriented Reforms

Eastern Europeans are generally convinced that their legacy is "postcommunist" and as such it has some features that distinguish it crucially from the "postauthoritarian" heritage found elsewhere (Bruszt, 1989; Comisso, Dubb, and Metigue 1991). The basic argument is that while in other parts of the world the establishment of capitalism preceded the transition to democracy, in Eastern Europe the transition to democracy launched the transition to capitalism. Hence, the argument continues, the problems facing Eastern European countries are qualitatively different from those confronting other parts of the world. Specifically, Eastern European countries do not have either market institutions or the bourgeoisie.

Yet the issue is whether, at least in the economic realm, these labels do not hide some essential similarities. If one delves beneath the labels, one sees that the state was weak as an organization in Eastern Europe and in Latin America, that the relation between the state and the public firms in Eastern Europe was not qualitatively different from that between the state and large private and public firms in Latin America, and that the differences in state regulation of prices and allocation of resources were only of degree (Przeworski 1991). Both Latin American and Eastern European countries were characterized by overgrown bureaucracies and weak revenue-collecting systems, and both sets of countries experienced a fiscal crisis that in some places expressed itself in hyperinflation. Indeed, one powerful argument in favor of similarities is that the economic reforms launched in Eastern Europe differ little from those attempted in Latin America.

These reforms – we will refer to them as "market-oriented" – comprise various mixtures of measures designed to stabilize the economy, steps oriented to change its structure, and at times sales of public assets. The central purpose of stabilization is to slow down inflation and improve the financial position of the state. The central goal of structural reforms is to increase the efficiency of resource allocation. The aim of privatization is less clear, since ostensible reasons for the sale of public assets are not always the true ones. Yet even if all these measures are successful in their own terms, their effect on reviving economic growth is not immediately apparent. While particular reform programs differ in scope and pace, stabilization and, in particular, structural reforms, necessarily cause a temporary decline of consumption. Even when accompanied by incomes policies, stabilization must entail a transitional reduction of demand, due to a combination of reduced public spending and high interest rates. Trade liberalization, antimonopoly measures, reductions of subsidies to industries and prices inevitably cause temporary unemployment of capital and labor. Privatization implies reorganization: again a costly transition. Moreover, market-oriented reforms are often undertaken when the effects of the original shock are still present (Brada and King, 1992) and while some important markets are still missing.[32] Finally, architects of reforms make mistakes, and mistakes are costly. Hence, in the short run the effect of economic reforms on growth must be negative.[33] Indeed, for proponents of reforms, unemployment and firm closings constitute evidence that reforms are effective: if unemployment failed to rise to between 8 and 10 percent in 1991, the former Czechoslovak economics minister, Vladimir Dlouhy, said, "It would be a sign that the reforms were not working" (*Financial Times*, 6 February 1991). Reform programs are thus caught between the faith of those who foresee their ultimate effects and the skepticism of those who experience only their immediate consequences.

This is why interim evaluations of reform programs tend to be highly inconstant and controversial. Given that market-oriented reforms inevitably entail a transitional decline in consumption, it is not apparent how to judge their success. There are three ways to think about "success." The first, followed by Nelson (1990) and most of her collaborators, is to define it merely in terms of a continued implementation of reform measures, whatever they may be: they gave up on using economic criteria to evaluate the success of reforms and decided to explain instead "the degree to which policy decisions were carried out rather than economic outcomes of the measures taken." The second, implicit in most economic literature and in Haggard and Kaufman (1992), is in terms of stabilization and liberalization. The third, to which we adhere, is to remain skeptical until an economy exhibits growth under democratic conditions.

The first conception is untenable, since it is based on the assumption that whatever measures had been introduced, they must have been appropriate. This conception admits no possibility of policy mistakes and – the point bears repetition – such mistakes are frequent and perhaps inevitable. The choice of the anchor (the nominal quantity on which the stabilization program rests, such as exchange rate, interest rate, or money emission), the sequencing of deregulatory measures (capital account versus trade first), the method and timing of devaluations, and the distribution of cuts of public expenditures are not obvious. There is no such thing as *the* sound economic blueprint, only alternative hypotheses, to be tested in practice and at a cost. Indeed, the sequencing of reform strategies evokes sharp disagreements and, as the Chilean debacle of 1982 demonstrates, wrong decisions lead to costly mistakes.

The second conception is safer but is still based on the conjecture that stability and competition are sufficient to generate growth: a conjecture we believe false. This posture assumes that the partial steps would eventually lead to growth and prosperity. Yet this is but a conjecture. Inflation may be arrested by a sufficient dose of recession, but the evidence that successful stabilization leads to restored growth is weak. Opening the economy and increasing exports may result in improved creditworthiness of a country, but the only beneficiaries may be the foreign creditors. The sale of public firms may fill state coffers, but the revenues can be stolen or squandered. Thus, the causal links between the particular reform measures and their ultimate goal remain flimsy. As Remmer (1986:7) reported with regard to the IMF Standby Programs, there is "only a moderate correlation between the implementation of IMF prescriptions and the achievement of desired economic results."

If the ostensible purpose of market-oriented reforms is to increase material welfare, then these reforms must be evaluated by their success in generating economic growth. Anything short of this criterion is just a restatement of the neoliberal hypothesis, not its test. Given that the reform process entails intertemporal trade-offs, conjectures about distant consequences cannot be avoided. Yet unless we insist on thinking in terms of growth, we risk suffering through a long period of tension and deprivation only to discover that the strategy that generated them was erroneous. The argument that "the worse, the better" cannot be maintained indefinitely; at some time things must get better. The ultimate economic criterion for evaluating the success of reforms can only be whether a country resumes growth at stable, moderate levels of inflation.

While economic reforms have been pursued by some authoritarian regimes and by some well-established democracies, newly established democratic regimes simultaneously face the urgent needs of overcoming an economic crisis and of consolidating the nascent institutions. Hence, the political criterion of successful reforms must be the consolidation of democracy. And if reforms are to proceed under democratic conditions, distributional conflicts must be institutionalized: all groups must channel their demands through the democratic institutions and abjure other tactics. Regardless of how pressing their needs may be, political forces must be willing to subject their interests to the verdict of representative institutions. They must be willing to accept defeats and to wait, confident that these institutions will continue to offer opportunities the next time around. They must adopt the institutional calendar as the temporal horizon of their actions, thinking in terms of forthcoming elections, contract negotiations, or at least fiscal years. They must assume the stance put forth by John McGurk, the chairman of the British Labour Party, in 1919:

We are either constitutionalists or we are not constitutionalists. If we are constitutionalists, if we believe in the efficacy of the political weapon (and we do, or why do we have a Labour Party?) then it is both unwise and undemocratic because we fail to get a majority at the polls to turn around and demand that we should substitute industrial action. (Cited in Miliband 1975: 69)

Regardless of their age, democracies persist whenever all the major political forces find that they can improve their situation if they channel their demands and their conflicts within the democratic institutions. The reason new democracies are more vulnerable is that, as we have seen, institutional issues often remain unresolved for a long period after a particular democratic system has been installed. Since the choice of institutions is often problematic and conflictual when a dictatorship falls, often the conflict about the institutional framework remains open, or some institutions are adopted just as an interim solution. These institutional frameworks are frequently inappropriate for the specific political and economic conditions. Moreover, as Hardin (1987) has argued, habituation plays an important role in inducing political actors to stay within the existing institutional framework: constitutions are often "contracts by convention."

Hence, democratic institutions can be consolidated only if they offer the politically relevant groups incentives to process their demands within the institutional framework. But economic reforms tend to engender a transitional decline in consumption. This is then the source of the dilemma faced by new democracies: how to create incentives for political forces to process their interests within the democratic institutions when material conditions continue to deteriorate?

Evidence

If success means resuming growth under democratic conditions, the evidence for successful recipes turns out to be thin. The case that established at least the possibility of success as we define it is Spain, which underwent a painful period of industrial reconversion yet irreversibly consolidated democratic institutions. This experience is paralleled by Portugal after 1983 and perhaps Uruguay. Chile is growing under democratic conditions, but the reform process, undertaken by an exceptionally repressive military regime, was long and its economic and social costs were enormous. South Korea underwent a successful stabilization in 1981 with some slowdown of growth, but it has been growing at a relatively rapid pace before and after. Mexico, with its peculiar political regime, has been attentive to social costs and may be on the brink of resumed growth, not yet under democratic institutions. Finally, among the Eastern European countries, incomes have tumbled since 1989 in all countries regardless of their reform strategies, and only in Poland has this decline been arrested by 1992.

These cases are so varied that it is not easy to determine to what extent their success has been due to policies or to circumstances. Spain did not face the need to stabilize, while the rates of inflation in Portugal, South Korea, Mexico, and Hungary have been quite moderate by the standards of Argentina, Bolivia, Brazil, Poland, or Yugoslavia. Foreign debt was an overriding consideration in the case of Argentina, Bolivia, Brazil, Mexico, Hungary, Poland, and former Yugoslavia but not in southern Europe. And the scope of reforms differed from country to country, variously combining measures aimed at stabilization, liberalization, and industrial reconversion. Hence, we do not pretend to have established the conditions for success: there is just not enough historical experience to permit a solid empirical evaluation of the approach we propose.

Our three main hypotheses are (1) that stabilization and liberalization are not sufficient to generate growth unless these reforms are targeted to redress the fiscal crisis and to generate public savings, (2) that without a social policy, political conditions for the continuation of reforms become eroded, and (3) that technocratic style of policy making weakens the nascent democratic institutions.

Before we examine these hypotheses, a comment is required concerning stabilization policies. Bresser Pereira (1993) argues that these policies often fail because they do not redress the "fundamentals," but also because they misdiagnose the causes of inflation and induce unnecessary social costs. This analysis is now widely shared. On the one hand, trying to stop inflation purely by controlling nominal quantities is absurd: without first correcting fundamentals, which include above all the fiscal crisis of the state, heterodox policies simply postpone fiscal adjustment. On the other hand, inflation is often inertial. And, as Bruno (1991: 2) observes, given the inertial character of inflation, "The orthodox cure is necessary but not sufficient. The correction of fundamentals does not by itself remove inflationary inertia. . . . Supplementary direct intervention in the nominal process, such as a temporary freeze of wages, prices, and the exchange rate, can substantially reduce the initial cost of disinflation." Correcting the fundamentals includes restructuring the flows of government expenditures and revenues as well as reducing the stocks of foreign and domestic debt. Breaking the spiral of inflation calls for policies targeted at nominal quantities, including incomes policies. Without correcting the fundamentals, stabilization policies are likely to be ineffective; without heterodox policies they will also be inefficient: relying exclusively on the reduction of demand to break inflation engenders unnecessarily high social costs.

To examine the effect of market-oriented reforms on growth, we need to distinguish three questions: (1) Why do stabilization and liberalization (of foreign trade and domestic competition) induce recessions? (2) Why do some stabilization programs undermine future growth? (3) Are stability and competition sufficient for a resumption of growth?

Stabilization programs tend to induce profound recessions, even when they are not accompanied by liberalization. The reason is at least twofold: (1) stabilization is usually achieved by reducing demand, and (2) interest rates tend to soar beyond the targeted level during stabilization. The mechanism that leads to excessive interest rates depends on the anchor that is being used (Blanchard et al. 1991), but one common effect is that a successful stabilization makes money more attractive, and the increased demand for money cannot be met by increased monetary emission without rekindling inflation. Another reason interest rates remain high is that credit is being rationed. In turn, the reduction of subsidies to industries and of prices, as well as the reduction of import tariffs and domestic antimonopoly measures, sharply lower rates of return and cause unemployment of capital and labor. Among the cases of successful stabilization,[34] unemployment increased sharply in Bolivia after 1985;[35] it climbed from 9.7 percent in 1974 to 16.8 percent in 1976 in Chile, from 5.1 percent in 1984 to 7.1 percent in 1986 in Israel, from zero in 1989 to over 15 percent in 1993 in Poland, while in South Korea, the capacity utilization rate fell from 77.5 percent in 1980 to 69.4 percent by 1983.

While high interest rates may be transitory, their effect lasts beyond the stabilization period. When interest rates remain exorbitant during a protracted period, not only "bad" but also "good" firms go under. As Fischer (1991: 404–405) pointed out, "Investment will not resume until real interest rates reach a reasonable level, and prolonged periods of high real interest rates create financial crises and bankruptcies even for firms that would be viable at reasonable levels of interest rate." Or, in Frenkel's (1991: 403) words, "Stabilization efforts are often associated with extremely high real rates of interest, which discourage investment and hamper growth." Indeed, to consider again only the cases of successful stabilization, in Bolivia private investment declined from the already minuscule level of 3.8 percent of GDP in 1984 to 2.7 percent in 1985 and to 2.5 percent four years later; in Chile, it fell from 8.7 percent of GDP in 1974 to 3.9 percent in 1975 and surpassed the prestabilization level only three years later; in Israel, gross investment (private and public) fell by 10.6 percent in 1985, recuperated the year later, and began to decline again by 1988; in Poland total investment fell by 1992 to 62.8 percent of the prereform level. Only in those countries that enjoyed a reversal of capital flight did private investment continue to grow at a rapid pace throughout the stabilization period.

The second reason stabilization programs often undermine the prospects for future growth has been highlighted by Tanzi (1989) in an autocritique of IMF prescriptions: the expenditure cuts, inherent in the attempt to cope with the fiscal crisis, tend not to discriminate between government consumption and public investment. And, having cited several instances in which stabilization policies undermined the capacity for growth, Tanzi (1989: 30) concluded:

In all these examples, the *supply* has been reduced, thus creating imbalances that, in time, have manifested themselves as excessive demand. In these cases, demand-management policies alone would have reduced the symptoms of these imbalances but would not have eliminated the causes. Thus, stabilization programs might succeed stabilization programs without bringing about a durable adjustment.

Indeed, investment projects are often politically easier to cut than government consumption services or public employment. Both the public infrastructural investments and measures to induce private investment are reduced, thus reducing future supply. The evidence of the successful stabilization experiences is uniform: in Bolivia, public investment declined from 8.4 percent in 1984 to about 3.0 percent after 1985; in Chile, it fell from 12.5 percent in 1974 to 4.8 percent in 1983 and rose again to 7.1 percent by 1985;[36] in

Mexico it declined by 13.4 percent in 1987 and continued to decline thereafter; in Eastern Europe, except Hungary, public investment simply collapsed.

Neither the observation that stabilization entails a recession nor even that stabilization programs often undermine conditions for future growth is now controversial: indeed, the voices we have cited emanate from the World Bank and the IMF. Where we depart from the neoliberal consensus is with regard to the point central in Bresser Pereira's (1993) analysis: we argue that market-oriented reforms are not sufficient to generate conditions for growth.

Admittedly, the empirical evidence is inconclusive. In Bolivia, the total GDP declined during the year following stabilization and then grew anemically, while per capita GDP continued to fall through 1990. In Chile, GDP tumbled by 12.9 percent in 1975; growth resumed until the great crash of 1982, when GDP fell by 14.1 percent, and resumed again after 1985. In Israel, GDP (business sector only) actually grew during stabilization but became stagnant three years later. In Mexico, signs of a recovery are evident, but per capita growth continues to be anemic. In South Korea, growth slowed down but continued to be high by comparative standards. In Eastern Europe, GDP continues to decline.[37] Systematic reviews of evidence generate mixed conclusions. Williamson (1990: 406) showed that among ten Latin American countries that had pursued "full or partial" reforms, four were growing in 1988–1989 while six were stagnant or declining; among eleven countries which did not pursue reforms or undertook them only recently, one was growing and ten were stagnant or declining: a positive but not an overwhelming correlation. Blanchard et al. (1991: 61) reported that "looking at the post-stabilization performance of countries that have stabilized, one concludes that in most cases, economic growth has returned only gradually and unimpressively." A recent analysis by the IMF (1992) shows a more positive picture, but its methodology leaves much to be desired. In turn, a World Bank evaluation of the effects of adjustment lending generated highly skeptical conclusions about its effect on private investment and growth (Faini et al. 1989).

Clearly, these patterns lend themselves to differing assessments, particularly when they are juxtaposed to the experience of countries that continue to suffer from a fiscal crisis and high rates of inflation. Yet the issue here is not whether countries that underwent a successful stabilization perform better than countries where stabilization attempts have failed or have not been pursued. The question is whether a successful stabilization, even when combined with other market-oriented reforms, is sufficient to generate growth. And since the experiments are continuing, one can always argue that in some future it will.

Given the paucity of evidence, it is useful to review theoretical arguments. The neoliberal assumption – "the Washington consensus" (Williamson 1990) – that underlies the program of market-oriented reforms is that once stability and competition are achieved, growth will follow. Yet, perhaps surprisingly, this neoliberal posture has shaky foundations even in neoclassical economic theory.

Neoclassical economic theory has little to say about growth.[38] Its preoccupations are mainly static. And anyone who has read Schumpeter knows that static efficiency is a poor criterion of welfare. Dynamic economies are not efficient in the static sense: they use a number of techniques, with different cost–benefit ratios. In turn, the issue of whether a competitive market generates dynamic efficiency is already more complex. The theory of economic growth that emerged from neoclassical economics, the Solow–Swan model of exogenous growth, argued that competitive equilibrium is efficient, but it leads to stagnation of income in the absence of exogenous population growth and exogenous technical change. Recent models do provide an endogenous explanation of economic growth, but in these theories the competitive equilibrium is no longer efficient (Lucas 1988; Barro 1990; Becker, Murphy, and Tamura 1990; Romer 1990). The "engine of growth" in these models is externalities, whether in education, skills, technology, or whatever. And competitive markets, in which firms do not capture full return to their endowments, undersupply the factors that generate such externalities.

In sum, the present state of economic theory does not support the conclusion that stability and competition are sufficient to generate growth. Whether one takes the theory of incomplete markets, with their informational asymmetries, or the theory of endogenous growth, with constant returns to a single factor and externalities, or the theory of non-Walrasian trade, one will discover arguments that stability and competition are not sufficient for growth.

At the very least, economic reforms are a protracted process. Moreover, they necessarily induce a temporary reduction of consumption for an important part of the population. Even if the stabilization-liberalization programs are designed with a view toward resumed growth and even if the state adopts appropriate development strategies, the period between stabilization and the resumption of growth is inevitably long. Edwards and Edwards (1991: 219) estimate eight to ten years as the lag to be expected. Solimano (1992) shows that it takes from two to seven years before inflation rate subsides below 25 percent per year and five to six years before investment begins to increase. Bruno noted that commodity and labor markets can take three to four years to adjust to changes[39] (reported in *IMF* 1993: 40). In the meantime, per capita consumption will decline or stagnate, and some incomes will be pushed below the threshold of absolute poverty. And if people are to make intertemporal trade-offs, if they are to accept a transitional reduction of consumption and to be impervious to "populist" appeals, they must have confidence that the temporary sacrifices will lead to an eventual improvement of their own material conditions. The policy style, about which more is said later, is an important factor in shaping this confidence. But even more important is that the imminent danger people face not threaten their livelihood: people whose physical survival is imperiled cannot think about the future. They have no intertemporal trade-offs to make – hence, the political importance of social policies that protect at least the basic incomes during the period of transition.

Citizens of new democracies expect to enjoy social as well as political rights. Demands for the satisfaction of "social citizenship" – in T. H. Marshall's (1964: 76) words, "a kind of basic human equality associated with the concept of full membership of a Community" – require that security and opportunity be shared by all. Social policies respond to these demands through the provision of health and education and through income maintenance. This provision is generally limited when new democracies venture on the path of economic reforms: this is why short-term effects of stabilization and liberalization threaten the basic livelihood of those most adversely affected by the steps toward market economy. The question is whether these steps will be continued as a verdict of the democratic process.

The typical argument of economists – that the economic blueprint is "sound" and only irresponsible "populists" undermine it[40] – is just bad economics. A sound economic strategy is one that addresses itself explicitly to the issue of whether reforms will be supported as the costs are experienced. At the least, reforms must be credible (Calvo 1989): it must be in the best interest of politicians to pursue the measures they announced once they obtain support for these measures. And credibility is not only a matter of economics: if policies are politically unsustainable, economic actors will not treat them as credible.

Our evidence concerning the political effects of social policies is extremely limited: we have one case, Spain, where social expenditures were considerably extended as industrial reconversion proceeded; one, Poland, where they were drastically cut as the country simultaneously undertook stabilization and liberalization; and some intermediate ones, notably Bolivia, which developed, with foreign assistance, a narrowly targeted program of employment for the miners who lost jobs, and Mexico, which developed a program of supporting food expenditures for the groups most adversely affected by the stabilization. The distinctive feature of Spain is that social policy was broad in scope – it comprised health, education, and income maintenance and it entailed qualitative changes in the system of self-government and delivery – and that this policy was accompanied by an active labor market intervention. Poland provides the clearest contrast: the preexisting system of social services disintegrated, social expenditures were drastically reduced, survival was left principally to charity, and labor market policy was limited to unemployment compensation. The political effect was that in Spain the Socialist Party, which led the reform process, continued to win elections without a serious social upheaval; in Bolivia, parties supporting the continuation of reforms won a majority in the 1989 presidential elections; while in Poland, parties advocating that reforms be continued won about 20 percent of the vote in the parliamentary elections of October 1991. Yet, since the initial conditions and the challenges facing these countries were quite different, it is impossible to treat even these cases as paired comparisons.

The Spanish social policy was sufficiently extensive that it could be conceptualized by the government and perceived by the population as progressing toward "social citizenship": a guarantee of a reasonably adequate and equal welfare protection for all members of the political community. This policy was financed by a significant increase of fiscal revenues, originating from progressive taxation and distributed through a decentralized system of regional self-government. As Maravall (1993) demonstrates, this experience of "social citizenship" was distinctly tied in Spain to the consolidation of political democracy: in spite of widespread unemployment, people have learned that political democracy brings social rights. As a result, one striking feature of the Spanish public opinion data is the gradual disassociation between the evaluations of the economic situation and those of political institutions.

Short of guaranteeing "social citizenship" to everyone regardless of their labor market status, there are three ways to secure basic incomes: one is to maintain full employment, another to assure everyone a minimum income, and the last to insure against unemployment. Active labor market and income insurance policies are thus to some extent substitutes. Command economies rely on the first method, market economies on different combinations of all three, often with incomplete coverage. The net of welfare services has been always rudimentary and fragmentary in poor capitalist countries, while it disintegrated along with central planning in the command economies.

Economic reforms cause unemployment: a new phenomenon among the command economies and an increasingly widespread one where markets had previously allocated jobs. When unemployment rises, basic income protection becomes the paramount concern of large segments of the population, several times larger than those actually unemployed at any particular moment.[41] Without a net of social protection and without income insurance, a loss of employment means the loss of livelihood. And this is a cost no one can tolerate even in the short run.

In the face of mounting unemployment, an active labor market policy is thus essential to reduce not only the economic but also the social costs of reforms. The neoliberal posture is based on the assumption that once the economy is deregulated and privatized and the conditions for competition are thereby created, markets will emerge, and their operation will cause resources to be reallocated across sectors and activities. Yet, first, markets do not "emerge" out of competition: they must be created by policy. Even if unemployment is only frictional or structural, an elaborate and costly system of institutions is required to orient the newly unemployed toward new opportunities.[42] Without a well-functioning labor market, resources will not be reallocated across sectors. Yet even when the basic markets are present, the reallocation of resources that is needed to make some economies efficient may be just too massive to take place without an extensive involvement of the state. To take just one case, albeit extreme, if Polish agriculture is to become as efficient as that in Western Europe, the number of persons dependent on agriculture would have to be reduced by about 20 percent of the labor force: at least 2.7 million people would have to be displaced. A transformation of this magnitude cannot take place overnight, and all the OECD countries massively support agriculture to avoid the social and political effects of the dislocation that exposing this sector to competition would entail.

To the extent that widespread unemployment persists during extended periods, some people find themselves without the means of livelihood, and many others live under a constant fear of losing jobs.[43] And the people who experience or feel threatened by unemployment are most likely to oppose reforms.[44] If their livelihood is not protected at least by narrowly targeted income insurance policies, this resistance may assume explosive forms.

The political impact of market-oriented reforms may depend on (1) the initial income distribution, (2) the distributional effect of reforms themselves, and (3) the scope of social policies. The effect of the initial income inequality is not obvious (Przeworski, 1991). Consider two countries, one as unequal as Brazil, where the top quintile earns twenty-seven times more than the bottom one, and one as equal as the former Soviet Union, and assume that the average income in both countries hovers slightly above poverty. Now, suppose that as a result of reforms, average income temporarily declines somewhat without any change in the distribution. Then the proportion of the newly poor will be small in the income-unequal country, whereas in the income-equal country everyone might find themselves in poverty. This seems to have been the experience of Russia, where, as of 1992, 61.3 percent of the population was estimated to be under the poverty line (UNICEF 1994). If the newly poor constitute the group most vociferously resisting reforms, then reforms are more likely to succeed politically in the initially less egalitarian country.

Our knowledge of the distributional effects of reforms is limited. On a priori grounds, it can be expected that unemployment will hit the less skilled workers in some sectors and public employees, while the real value of pensions and other transfers will decline. The phenomenon of the *déclassement* of the middle class – declines of income that change class position when, for example, people are forced to move from an apartment to a *favela* – can be expected to be most explosive politically, while the less educated, older, and socially isolated groups may be unable to express their reactions politically.

Social policies face the familiar dilemma between their political effects and their economic costs. On the one hand, universalistic policies are politically more popular precisely because they are universalistic. But they are expensive, and when the level of provision is not sufficient to be effectively universal, access to social services has to be rationed through administrative procedures that often deteriorate into clientilism and patronage (Moene and Wallerstein 1992). On the other hand, targeted, means-tested policies are cheaper but politically unpopular: they are often perceived as gifts to those who do not want to work. Since universalistic policies entail a willingness to pay higher taxes, at least within some range, policies that go a long way toward but stop short of universalism seem optimal in generating political support.

Admittedly, our evidence that the absence of social protection, whether in the form of a broad social policy or targeted income support schemes, translates into an effective political opposition against economic reforms is again very thin: it relies on the juxtaposition of Spain and Poland.[45] Yet the Polish case – the only one where we were able to study the political dynamic at the micro level – seems most suggestive (Przeworski 1993a). In Poland, the fear of unemployment turned people against the reform plan and overwhelmed all the beneficial effects about which most people were convinced.[46] If market-oriented reforms fail in Poland for political reasons – and this possibility is real – it will be because unemployment was introduced without a net of social protection. But we are aware that the causal chain that leads from individual discontent to organized reactions against the effects of reforms and from organized reactions to their abandonment is contingent and complex: reforms may well continue against popular resistance, even under democratic institutions.

This point brings us to our third and final hypothesis: that technocratic policy style weakens the nascent democratic institutions. The generic dilemma facing governments that embark on the path of reform is that broad consultation with diverse political forces may lead to inertia, while reforms imposed from above may be impossible to implement in the face of political resistance and economic incredulity. Faced with this dilemma, governments can adopt four different policy styles:

1. Convinced about the need for immediate reforms, persuaded about the technical soundness of the economic blueprint, and equipped with decree powers, the executive may force reform measures on the society. This *decretismo* is so widespread that it seems almost inherent in the neoliberal approach: an overwhelming proportion of legal acts concerning the economy in Argentina, Brazil, and Peru consists of presidential decrees. The decrees need not and often do not correspond to programs advocated by the victorious candidates in election campaigns: from Paz Estenssoro in Bolivia to Fujimori in Peru, recent years have witnessed several cases when victorious candidates embraced the content and style of reforms against which they vigorously campaigned.

2. When the executive has no decree powers but enjoys a majority in the legislature, the same technocratic style appears as "mandatism." As Margaret Thatcher often observed, she had told the people what she would do if elected; they voted for her, and she had the mandate to do what she thought appropriate; people would have a chance to decide whether this was indeed what they wanted in the next election. This style is still technocratic since beyond the electoral campaign it entails no consultation with opposing political forces in Parliament and no concertation with forces outside it, at the stages either of policy formulation or of implementation.

3. "Parliamentarism" is a policy style that can result either from a deliberate decision by the majority to consult and negotiate with some opposing

forces in the legislature or, frequently, from the fact that proportional representation systems fail to generate majorities, thus making coalitions and compromises inevitable. While the government enjoys some autonomy, it consults and negotiates at various steps along the way, making public the policy options and the conflicting views. Political support is thus organized as policies are formulated and implemented; indeed, when no party has a majority, policies can be pursued only if they maintain the approval of some coalition.

4. Finally, "corporatism," or perhaps better "concertation," is a policy style that extends consultation and negotiation beyond the parliamentary actors, to unions, employers' associations or other interest groups.

Our hypothesis is that policy styles matter. One should distinguish, however, three considerations. First, consultation and concertation may serve to improve the technical quality of reform programs. We realize that this is an unorthodox view, since the usual argument is that having to negotiate the economic program undermines its logical coherence. Yet this argument assumes that the program is coherent and free from mistakes to begin with, and we have already seen that this is a questionable assumption. Neither the logical consistency of any particular reform strategy nor the design of specific measures are obvious even to professional economists, and in fact, many important decisions are made in a haphazard way when they are hidden from public scrutiny.[47] Moreover, professional economists give advice to opposing political parties, and even unions: their voices can serve to warn about impending mistakes.

Second, discussion and negotiation may serve to build political bases of support for the particular reform strategy. If the program is forged in negotiations with diverse political forces, it will emerge in a form that will be easier for these forces to support. Such a program may retard the pace of reforms and may eliminate the element of surprise necessary for some stabilization measures, such as freezes, price deregulations or capital levies. Yet, to argue one more time against prevailing opinions, such a program may be more, not less, credible, because it creates political conditions for the continuation of reforms. Contrary to frequent announcements by technocrats that they will proceed regardless of political pressures upon them, decrees are often simply ineffective precisely because economic agents anticipate that the particular policies are politically unsustainable. Policy making by decree signals that the government has no political capability of resolving the fiscal crisis and that it has a short time horizon over which it feels confident it can make economic policies. Hence, policy by decree does not offer the credibility that is required for investment that entails sunk costs (Rodrik 1991).

Finally, if one cares about democracy, one must take the political criterion as autonomous. Policy styles matter because they have the effect of channeling political conflicts and of teaching political actors where the real locus of power is located. The Polish experience is eloquent (Przeworski 1993a). Most decisions were made outside the framework of the representative institutions, and people quickly learned that this is how they are made: repeated surveys show that people do not see the locus of power in the properly constituted institutions. Consultation and negotiation among representative organizations within the framework of representative institutions is necessary to channel political conflicts toward them. If decisions are made elsewhere, representative institutions wilt.

Hence, we find that subjecting the reform strategy to the competitive interplay of political forces is superior on all the three grounds: it improves policy, it builds support for the continuation of reforms, and it helps consolidate democratic institutions. Yet our advocacy of this policy style must be tempered in several important ways.

First, even if a government is eager to consult and negotiate, it is by no means a given that it will find willing partners. The dominant strategy of the opposition may be to let the government make its mistakes, so that it will become unpopular and lose elections. Sharing the responsibility for a socially costly program as a minor partner may turn out to be politically costly. The Portuguese Social Democrats were willing to bet on this strategy and experienced a spectacular electoral success as a result, but the unions in Argentina repeatedly rejected overtures from the Radical Party government. Moreover, excessive consensus is also threatening to democracy: some political forces should monitor the government from an adversarial position. It is essential that some political parties, motivated by the desire to win elections, monitor the performance of the government.

Second, since the combination of left-wing partisan control with institutionalized concertation between unions and employers' associations is generally found to generate superior economic performance among the OECD countries, a question emerges whether this policy style would not also be more successful in the case of new democracies. Yet this question is largely irrelevant, since the organizational preconditions for this policy style are absent in the countries we consider. Most importantly, unions are too weak and too decentralized to serve as a partner in concertation.[48] And since in many new democracies employers' associations enjoy a disproportionate political influence through informal channels and tend to vigorously oppose some essential elements of reform, notably trade liberalization and tax increases, concertation may result in undermining reforms.

Another way to pose the issue of policy style is to ask whether a "strong" or a "weak" government is more likely to be successful in seeing reforms to the end. These are, however, ambiguous terms. Some governments that appear strong because they issue decrees without previously building the political bases of support end up simply ineffective: the experience of Collor de Mello is the prime example. In turn, minority governments, forced to build coalitions before they can launch a reform program, may turn out to be highly successful: witness the Socialist–Social Democratic government in Portugal. To make these terms more precise, we must distinguish between constitutional constraints, which bind all governments, and the conjunctural outcomes of elections, which determine the majority or minority status of particular officeholders. A government may be "weak" in the sense of not being constitutionally enabled to make some decisions (because it must go through the legislative process, because legislation is subject to judicial review, or because some decisions are reserved to autonomous institutions, such as the central bank) or it may be "weak" politically, incapable of legislating without first persuading its own party or without building coalitions of several parties.

We have argued in fact in favor of institutional structures that compel governments to discuss and negotiate while formulating and implementing policies. We see decree power as ineffectual economically and dangerous politically, and we see both political and institutional constraints as tempering technocratic proclivities. Yet, as Maravall (1993) demonstrates, policy styles are not uniquely determined either by the institutional framework or by the majority status of governments, and given again the paucity of successful cases, the empirical evidence appears inconclusive. Moreover, we do not question the fact that governments cannot spend all their time consulting and negotiating: they must have the power to govern. Nor do we underestimate the danger of self-serving, narrowly based opposition to reforms. Several sectors of society, notably firms that enjoy oligopolistic rents, the bourgeoisie that resists fiscal pressure, employees in the public sector, low-skilled workers in the private sector, various groups that traditionally enjoyed entrenched privileges, and, in some countries, peasants, may see their interests hurt as the result of reforms. Separately or in often strange alliances they resist reforms. Yet the idea that this resistance can be beaten to the punch, that reforms can be implemented so swiftly that these groups will not have time to organize and make their voices heard, that the program must be concluded before "political fatigue" sets in – this technocratic posture – is unfeasible, counterproductive with regard to the prospect of continued reforms, and risky for democracy.

Indeed, a central reason the opposition to reforms often assumes the form of defending short-term special interests is that these reforms are not a product of a political interplay among representative organizations within the terrain of representative institutions. Proponents of reforms should not fear democratic institutions. This fear is largely unfounded: while we still understand little about the microfoundations of individual postures with regard to reform programs, there is overwhelming evidence that such programs enjoy widespread support when they are launched, even if it is known that they will induce hardships. The Balcerowicz plan in Poland, the first Collor plan in Brazil, the Cavallo plan in Argentina, and even the Fujimori program in Peru enjoyed overwhelming support in public opinion polls (Przeworski 1993b; *Folha da Sao Paulo,* various issues; Stokes 1993). If the representative system were allowed to process conflicts about reforms, it is most likely that only a reasonable difference of opinions and responsible conflicts of interest would emerge: not a threat to the idea of reform as such, but only to the specific blueprint. By stifling public discussion, the specter of "populist reaction" serves mainly to defend particular groups of technocrats against alternative conceptions and competing teams.

Yet, since the neoliberal strategy entails significant social costs, reforms tend to be initiated from above and launched by surprise, independently of public opinion and without the participation of organized political forces. They tend to be adopted by decree or rammed through legislatures without modifications that would reflect the divergence of interests and opinions. The political style of implementation tends to be autocratic; governments seek to demobilize their own supporters rather than compromise their program through public consultation. In the end, the society learns that it can vote but not choose; legislatures believe that they have no role to play in policy elaboration; and the nascent political parties, trade unions, and other organizations perceive that their voices do not count. Hence, the autocratic policy style characteristic of neoliberal reforms tends to undermine representative institutions, to personalize politics, and to generate a climate in which policies are reduced to fixes, to a search for redemption. Even if neoliberal reform packages made good economics, they are likely to generate voodoo politics. Either the executive, impatient with the political process, decides to ram the reforms through by closing other branches of the government, as in Peru, or the opposition to reforms assumes an extraparliamentary form, as in Venezuela.

These consequences are not inevitable. Indeed, one reason why the opposition to reforms assumes nondemocratic forms is that democracy is incomplete to begin with. In a country with constitutional provisions that force the executive to seek legislative approval for policies before they are launched, with effective representative institutions and widespread political participation, governments cannot initiate reforms without first mustering support. Reforms would have to emerge from consultations channeled through the representative institutions. It is precisely the strength of democratic institutions, not exhortations by technocrats, that reduces the political space for the pursuit of immediate particularistic interests, for "populism." "Populism" is to a large extent an endogenous product of technocratic policy styles.

An Alternative Strategy

Even given all the caveats about the paucity of evidence, we are ready to summarize our analysis in a more prescriptive fashion, as a strategy. We support reforms aimed at stabilization, principally a reduction of the fiscal crisis with all its attendant consequences, because we see such reforms as inevitable once an economy enters an inflationary spiral. Moreover, we believe that an increased reliance on markets, national and international, to allocate resources is required to enhance efficiency in economies that are monopolistic, overregulated, and overprotected. We do not believe that such reforms can be pursued without a temporary decline of consumption, a rise in unemployment, or other social costs. Yet we have been critical of the standard neoliberal recipes since we believe that they are faulty in three fundamental ways: they induce economic stagnation, they incur unnecessarily large social costs, and they weaken the nascent democratic institutions. This is why we seek to offer an alternative approach to market-oriented reforms.

This approach consists of three recommendations. First, social policy must be elaborated and put in place as stabilization or liberalization is launched. Second, the entire reform package must minimize the transitional social costs and must be designed with a view toward resumed growth. Finally, reform programs should be formulated and implemented as a result of a political interplay of representative organizations within the framework of the representative institutions.

A social policy designed to protect everyone from the most dire effects must be an intrinsic part of any reform strategy that would be politically credible under democratic conditions. Spain underwent a decade of unemployment hovering around 16 percent, and approaching 22 percent in 1985, while the government repeatedly won elections, thanks to a broad political support that was to some extent due to the absence of credible political alternatives but also because of a considerable expansion of social policies: social expenditure increased from 9.9 percent of GDP in 1975 to 17.8 percent in 1989. This expansion of social expenditures reduced the risk of reforms for the groups hurt most drastically by the reform process and convinced people that the extension of social citizenship is a credible promise of democracy. And while the economic crisis is too acute in many countries to follow the example of Spain, both labor market institutions and basic-income protection schemes must be put in place as reforms that cause unemployment and reduce consumption are initiated.

The labor market institutions must be appropriate for the distribution and the duration of unemployment. In countries with a large informal sector, they must facilitate access to the formal labor market or petty entrepreneurship. They must comprise an information system, perhaps a subsidized credit system to promote self-employment, and, where the housing market is thin, a relocation system. Income protection must be sufficient to cover basic needs and facilitate job search and retraining, without creating incentives to remain idle.

Stabilization policies should be efficient in the sense of minimizing transitional costs and must be highly attentive to the effect on growth. The expenditure cuts must discriminate between consumption and investment. In the spirit of Tanzi (1989), minimal public investment targets should be exempt from cuts, and following Blejer and Cheasty (1989), selective instruments that raise the rate of return to private investment should be preserved. Moreover, given the overwhelming evidence about the productive role of education, educational expenditures, and at least preventive health programs, should be treated as intrinsic aspects of public investment.

Although trade-offs are obviously involved in decisions about the expenditure of scarce resources, social expenditures cannot be considered only as costs. Within limits, they also stimulate economic growth by providing a broader market for producers. Of course, if public-sector finances are totally out of balance, such expenditures will fuel inflation, but in a state of recession, which faces most Latin American and all Eastern European countries, social policies can provide a much needed stimulus. Moreover, if we adopt a longer-term view, the central lesson of the endogenous growth theories and, indeed, one of a few robust statistical findings concerning the determinants of growth is the importance of education, whether measured in terms of school enrollment rates or stock indices, such as literacy (Barro 1989; Levine and Renelt 1991; Persson and Tabellini 1991) and, more broadly, knowledge. Primary education for women has particularly high returns in terms of per capita growth (World Bank 1991). And while no similar statistical studies seem to be available with regard to health expenditures, the *World Development Report 1991* (World Bank 1991: 53–55) cites extensive evidence about the productivity-increasing effects of health programs. Hence, stabilizations that occur at the cost of reducing expenditures on education and health are likely to be counterproductive with regard to growth.[49]

There is overwhelming evidence (Nelson 1990) that stabilization efforts are normally undertaken as a result of a fiscal crisis of the state. In several countries, the collapse of authoritarian regimes was accompanied by economic crises, caused typically by the exhaustion of state-led and inward-oriented strategies of development. The consequence, besides an increasing inefficiency of the entire economic system, was a fiscal crisis: in many countries, the state was financially bankrupt. By "fiscal crisis" we mean not only that the public deficit was chronic or the public debt excessive, but that the state lost the capacity to finance its debt in noninflationary terms. The erosion of public savings deprived the states of the capacity to pursue any kind of a policy. Hence, even though the regimes were in various shades authoritarian, the state became economically impotent.

To put it bluntly, reforms should have as a basic objective the recovery of public savings, so as to permit the resumption of public investment and the active role of the state in industrial and technological policies. If growth is to be resumed, the goal of the reform measures must be not only to reduce inflation and increase competition, but to restore the capacity of the state to mobilize savings and pursue development-oriented policies. Public investment is necessary to correct for market failures, maintain the physical infrastructure, and accumulate human capital, as well as to provide opportunities and incentives for private investment.

While public bureaucracies should be streamlined wherever they are excessive and public programs should be eliminated or reorganized when they are not efficient in delivering most urgently needed services, stabilization should rely on a reduction of current consumption but not of investment, and this reduction should be targeted, via the tax system or a one-shot capital levy, at those who can best afford it. This includes foreign creditors: in most countries, resumed growth is not feasible without a significant reduction of the external as well as the internal debt.

A tax reform that enforces compliance, broadens the income base, and significantly increases the effective rates of collection must thus be an intrinsic ingredient of the reform package. One reason is that a tax reform will constitute evidence that the distribution of burdens is equitable, but the immediate economic purpose is to raise state revenues instead of cutting those expenditures that support future growth. We are unimpressed by arguments about the marginal deadweight cost of taxation: empirical evidence is at best mixed[50] and the present tax rates in most new democracies are abominably low, much lower than in the OECD countries (Cheibub 1994). A recent study by the World Bank (1991: 82) shows that the rate of return to private investment projects rises from 10.7 percent when fiscal deficit is greater than 8 percent of GDP to 14.3 percent when the deficit is less than 4 percent. Hence, there is a possibility for a Pareto-improving increase of state revenues: the rate of private after-tax return can go up as the effective tax rate is raised. To cite Blejer and Cheasty (1989: 46), "A tax system which is uniform and predictable, and which is associated with prudent macroeconomic management, may make higher rates more acceptable than they would be in a tax system with many exemptions that is associated with a fiscal position perceived to be unsustainable in the longer run."[51] Most resistance to taxation reflects a problem of collective action on the part of the bourgeoisie: while there is evidence that a financially healthy state, capable of pursuing consistent policies, would induce higher rates of return to private investment, firms and their stockholders are engaged in a "war of attrition" by which they seek to shift the burden onto others (Alesina and Drazen, 1991).

State intervention in allocating resources across sectors and activities, judicious and narrowly targeted, is necessary to resume growth, and this intervention is possible only if the state is capable of mobilizing public savings. According to Blejer and Cheasty (1989: 45–47), the government should

aim to set its total tax revenues and its total expenditures (both current and capital) at levels that would yield an overall surplus, which could then be made available, on a competitive and nonconcessionary basis, to the private sector as well as to public enterprises. This would provide the government with a powerful and flexible tool that would facilitate . . . the efficient allocation of investment.[52]

Moreover, they argue:

The government could increase domestic savings by undertaking actions which increase the perceived rate of return on private sector investments. One way of doing this would be to invest directly in projects which would result in positive externalities to the private sector.

In the light of recent research, as summarized by Grossman (1990), the state should engage in infrastructural investments not supplied efficiently by private agents, and it should pursue measures that increase the rate of return to private projects. This role includes a selective industrial policy that would comprise preferential credit rates for high-technology industries, in which the market rate of return is much lower than the social rate, for projects that suffer from high costs of entry, substantial economies of scale, or steep learning curves, and for projects that potentially spill over across firms due to externalities and asymmetries of information between suppliers and buyers.

If these arguments are valid, economic growth requires a significant and sizeable role by the state. Barro (1990) showed that the present utility of future consumption or, equivalently under some conditions, the rate of growth are maximized when the share of the public productive sector in the output equals the marginal elasticity of public capital. Findlay (1990) presented a similar result with regard to public employment. Barro used 25 percent as a rough guess for the optimal size of the public capital stock, and Cheibub (1994) found statistically that this number is somewhere around 20 percent, depending on whether one includes education and defense. Hence, some intermediate role of public investment and employment – very far from 100 percent but also far from zero – is optimal for economic growth.

Finally, reform programs must be processed through the representative institutions. We have argued that the democratic process can improve the technical quality of reform policies and can furnish the bases for continued support for reform. Yet democracy is an autonomous value, for which many people bore sacrifices when they struggled against authoritarian regimes. The quality of the democratic process, perhaps less tangible than material welfare, affects the everyday life of individuals: it empowers them as members of a political community or deprives them of that power. And if democracy is to be consolidated, that is, if all political forces are to learn to channel their demands and organize their conflicts within the framework of the democratic institutions, these institutions must play a real role in shaping and implementing policies that influence their life conditions.

Hence, our approach to market-oriented reforms calls for orienting reforms toward growth, for protecting material welfare against the transitional costs of reforms, and for making full use of democratic institutions in the formulation and implementation of reform policies. We realize that each of these recommendations involves costs. Industrial policies, social policies, and political compromises cost money, and trade-offs are inevitable. We do not offer blueprints: the design of specific reform strategies must reflect local constraints, and the trade-offs must be determined by the democratic process. All we argue is that, to be successful, reforms must explicitly aim at growth, income security, and democracy.

6. Privatization and Its Alternatives

The Pitfalls of Large-Scale Privatization

Privatization programs are justified by their advocates on three grounds: (1) enhancing economic efficiency, (2) increasing government revenue, and (3) eliciting political support. We can classify privatization strategies along two dimensions: whether a given strategy advocates a fast or slow privatization, and whether it advocates privatization from below (spontaneous privatization) or from above (centrally directed privatization).

Of course, any typology is arbitrary. We choose this one because it enables us to focus on two crucial dimensions of economic-political transformation. Democratic institutions have their "institutional time." The pace and timing of privatization strategies have important implications for the mutual relations among the political institutions. If one wants to push through privatization as quickly as possible, presidential decree power is needed, and parliamentary debates are an obstacle. In turn, the issue of who directs the privatization program shapes the relation between the state and the economy. The Hayekian belief about "spontaneous order" has been used against all attempts to guide the privatization process through policy intervention from above,[53] except in the form of a general enabling law that would allow the private sector to grow spontaneously.

The debates about the pace of privatization are based on economic as well as political arguments. Advocates of slow privatization believe that state firms should be sold off gradually, after the new rules of economic behavior begin to emerge and after a more rational price system and a real business class has had time to develop. In contrast, the advocates of fast privatization argue that "the potential cost of overly rapid privatization must be traded off with the high cost of maintaining the present system in which state-owned enterprises lack clear incentives in the face of the market forces now being introduced in Eastern Europe" (Lipton and Sachs 1990: 297). Moreover, the argument for fast privatization is often political. As Lipton and Sachs declare, "We believe that unless hundreds of large firms in each country are brought quickly into the privatization process, the political battle over privatization will soon lead to stalemate in the entire process, with the devastating long-term result that little privatization takes place at all'' (p. 298). However, none of these strategies of privatization can achieve simultaneously the three objectives just mentioned.

First, let us consider spontaneous privatization, which requires only a general enabling law but not specific government decisions. One possible outcome of this strategy is a "nomenklatura buyout," an outcome incompatible with the objective of building political support: the public will not like letting yesterday's political elite become today's economic elite. This is exactly the force leading to the establishment of a central apparatus in charge of the privatization process in Hungary, Poland, and the former Czechoslovakia. Regarding a buyout by workers, another form of spontaneous privatization, there is also an issue of justice.[54] These two cases clearly show that Hayekian faith in spontaneous social order and its exclusion of any consciously directed social reform do not pass the test of building political support.

Second, let us consider the sale of enterprises, one by one, under the centrally directed privatization strategy. The selling price must be cheap due to several reasons. One is the "lemon problem"[55] of asymmetric information, which is particularly serious given the underdeveloped capital markets and the macroeconomic uncertainty. Another reason is the weak bargaining power of governments vis-à-vis potential buyers, since the government has a need to sell quickly in order to reduce the budget deficit, while buyers (both domestic and foreign) have the option of strategic delay. In turn, the low selling price has two consequences: the objective of increasing government revenue is only partially satisfied, and the objective of building political support is violated. In fact, the first director of the Hungarian State Property Agency was fired in part because of a public accusation that public assets were being sold too cheaply to the rest of the world.[56]

Moreover, the one-by-one selling strategy can lead to the privatization of only the most profitable enterprises, leaving the unhealthy firms in the hands of the government and thus further undermining the objective of increasing government revenues. Indeed, one can plausibly expect that the net effect of this strategy will actually be to reduce government revenue. This is so mainly because the tax system under the traditional centrally planned economy system was implicit. As McKinnon (1991: 122) observed, under this system:

There was no need for a general corporate profits or value-added tax, where the legal tax liabilities of enterprise were well defined. Calculating corporate depreciation allowances and debating whether interest payments should be deductible from taxable enterprise profits were not critical issues. Nor was any formalized personal income tax necessary. Because almost all workers were employed directly by state-owned enterprises, by keeping wages low the government effectively withheld a tax on personal income at the source.

After privatization, this old tax base will be eroded; however, due to the consideration of microeconomic incentives, the new tax rate will not be set too high, and tax holidays will be given to foreign companies. Moreover, any new tax system will take time to become effective. Therefore, although selling state-owned enterprises may raise some short-term revenues, the net effect on the state treasury might well be negative.[57]

One might tend to think that the former East Germany is in a better situation to implement this selling strategy. However, a closer look at the experience of Treuhand – the agency entrusted with the task of privatizing about 8,000 former state-owned enterprises in East Germany – indicates that similar difficulties have emerged. Due to the specific macroeconomic arrangement of German unification, "the majority of East German firms have negative value if they are operated, since their costs exceed their revenue" (Akerlof et al. 1991: 3). Under such conditions, even in East Germany the pace of privatization is slow: as of late February 1991, only 700 small firms had been sold off.

The East German case is symptomatic of a general point: the strategy of selling one firm at a time cannot work under an adverse macroeconomic environment. The recession caused by stabilization plans, such as the Balcerowicz Plan in Poland, deepened by the collapse of the Council for Mutual Economic Assistance in January 1991, is likely to lead to a situation in which there are not enough buyers.[58]

Since many Eastern European officials understand that the strategy of selling state enterprises one by one does not work under current macroeconomic conditions and may even lead to the reduction of government revenue, the third alternative, a general distribution of property rights in state enterprises via vouchers, is under consideration. Enhancing economic efficiency is the most important justification of this privatization strategy: the hope is that whatever governments sacrifice in the short run by forsaking the income from selling the firms, both government revenue and political support would eventually recover if economic efficiency is increased. It is with this faith that the second Polish Solidarity government and the former Czechoslovak governments have opted for the strategy of a free distribution of vouchers.

The free distribution of state assets through voucher schemes is the most innovative design of privatization in Eastern Europe.[59] Although it has been tried on a small scale in British Columbia, the scale of Eastern European free distribution is unprecedented.

At the moment of this writing, no privatization sale to voucher holders has yet been completed. Yet what strikes us about the proposed voucher scheme in Eastern Europe is the absence of any serious financial regulation. In the recent experiment with the voucher scheme in the former Czechoslovakia, some mutual funds have made promises to the public that would be impossible to fulfill short of a massive inflation. And, as the history of financial crises, from the South Sea Bubble in seventeenth-century England to the Great Depression of the 1930s has shown, this absence of financial regulation paves the way for massive fraud that may nullify the assumed gains of efficiency and equity. The potential efficiency and equity gains from the strategy of free distribution of vouchers is not significant enough to warrant the high risks of losing government revenue. A prudent government would not pursue this strategy.

Given the pitfalls of the three alternative strategies discussed, a reform of the state sector seems more urgent and realistic than any large-scale privatization. In general, the hopes attached to privatization are based on four mistaken assumptions: (1) that private ownership will by itself solve principal–agent problems, forcing managers to maximize profit; (2) that the market is a source of incentives for employees rather than information for managers; (3) that enough capital would be forthcoming to infuse investment into newly private firms; and (4) that privatization will automatically bring forth the managerial skills needed to run large firms in a market environment. The first two assumptions are based on the nineteenth-century model of capitalism. The former Polish finance minister, Leszek Balcerowicz, described privatization as follows:

A market economy based on a broad participation of different forms of private ownership permits the achievement of the highest – among all economic systems known in practice – degree of effectiveness in using material and spiritual resources of a society. It generates as a result the quickest improvement of the level of life of citizens. This is so because economizing costs, good organization of work, high quality of production, effective search for new markets as well as technical progress and development are in the interest of *the proprietors who direct the work of enterprises*. (Speech reproduced in *Gazeta Wyborcza*, 13 July 1990; italics added)

The third assumption requires only elementary accounting: given that private savings in Eastern Europe do not exceed 10 percent of capital stock and assuming that foreigners will buy at most another 10 percent, where is the rest of the capital to come from? The last assumption ignores the fact that managers must be trained, rather than, as Hayekians would have it, emerge from the process of natural selection. As a result, Poland spent two years arguing about privatization, while no one knows what is the status of state enterprises, which continue to produce about 75 percent of the industrial output.

This criticism of the current schemes for a massive privatization certainly does not imply that state ownership is the best form of proprietorship under all conditions. We all know that state enterprises in centrally planned economies operated under the "soft-budget constraint." But, in our view, the soft-budget constraint has more to do with the nature of the modern credit-based economy than with state ownership per se. In all modern economies, banks and their client firms are explicitly or implicitly insured by the government in order to avoid financial crises.[60] This insurance leads to the problem of moral hazard on the part of the insured: a form of a soft-budget constraint. It is the rules and regulations of the financial markets, rather than the legal definition of ownership per se, that keep the softness of budget constraints in the West within an acceptable limit. We are confident that the reform of the public sector, described later, will harden the budget constraints of enterprises.

Alternatives to Privatization

If existing capitalist economies based on private ownership work reasonably well in terms of allocative efficiency, then why experiment with something new? First, because for countries faced with introducing markets and the denationalization of state-owned firms, "something new" cannot be avoided. Contrary to the neo-Hayekian claims, the financial and legal institutions and practices of advanced capitalism are not "natural," but man-made, and were constructed painstakingly over centuries. Moreover, their final forms, in different national episodes of capitalist development, were path-dependent, so that a simple transplantation of these institutions to the present-day Eastern European countries may not succeed. Second, in the contemporary discussion on privatization, equity is usually tacked on as an afterthought, perhaps reflecting the view that capitalism's degree of efficiency, contrasted with a communist alternative, is so great as to more than compensate the losers for what would have been an equal share of a much smaller pie under that alternative. Yet with respect to equity (justice in income distribution), capitalism as we have known it does not work reasonably well, especially in countries at low levels of development.

Why is social democracy not an adequate cure for the inegalitarianism of capitalism? Perhaps, when it works, it is. Yet social democracy requires, we believe, rather special political circumstances that are absent in many countries in which privatization is the current strategy. Since it permits a powerful capitalist class to exist (over 90 percent of productive assets are privately owned in Sweden), there must be a strong and unified labor movement to win redistribution through taxes. It would be unrealistic to believe that tax concessions of this magnitude can be effected simply through electoral democracy without an organized labor movement, when capitalists organize or finance influential political parties. Even in the Scandinavian countries, strong apex labor organizations have been difficult to sustain, and social democracy is now on the decline (Moene and Wallerstein 1992). We believe that some variant of the proposals we describe later is politically feasible in the existing or former communist countries and in some of the developing countries, while social democracy may be politically difficult to achieve given the absence of encompassing and centralized labor organizations.

Are there, then, feasible alternatives that can guarantee a superior distribution of welfare, including a more equal distribution of income, to that attainable by privatization? We argue that such alternatives exist, and we believe they do in part because there are negative externalities associated with the high degree of concentration of ownership of productive assets that characterizes every actually existing capitalist economy. After outlining our proposals, we return to discuss these externalities.

The communist model induced economic failure because it was incapable of solving three principal–agent problems: the manager–worker problem, the planner–manager problem, and the public–planner problem. The first problem consisted in getting workers to work hard: earning higher wages was not as necessary as in a market economy because a large part of a workers' consumption basket was received as a direct distribution from the firm, and the competition for jobs was slight. The second problem consisted in getting managers to carry out the planner's production plan: this problem existed because firms did not have to compete with other firms to market their products, either because they held a monopoly position, or because retailing was not the task of the firm. Managers became bargaining adversaries, not agents, of planners. In turn, the planner (state bureaucrat) was not a perfect agent of the public at large because politics were not competitive: he did not owe his job to the public but to the party, which was only very imperfectly responsive to the public's desires.

Modern capitalism has its analogous principal–agent problems: the manager–worker problem, the stockholder–manager problem, and the public–stockholder problem. The worker–manager problem remains essentially the same; it is solved by using both the carrot and the stick. For instance, job ladders within the firm, with wages increasing as one moves up the ladder, are constructed to give workers an incentive to build a career in the firm. Another recent theory explains what is called the efficiency wage: a firm pays workers more than they are willing to accept, to make it costly for them to lose their jobs. Were the firm able to costlessly monitor the worker's performance, this would be unnecessary, but since such monitoring is prohibitively costly, the efficiency wage induces the worker to work hard and carefully even while not being watched, because it would be too costly to lose the job if caught shirking.

The analogue of the planner–manager agency problem under capitalism is the stockholder–manager problem. Managers are supposed to undertake policies that are in the best interest of the stockholders, that is, policies that maximize profits or the value of the firm. It is often not in the best personal interest of the manager to do so. Different capitalist countries have undertaken quite different strategies to solve this agency problem. It is believed by many U.S. finance economists that the stock market is the institution that forces managers to operate firms in the interests of shareholders. If profits decline because of bad management, the stock price of the firm falls, and it becomes an attractive target for a takeover by those who would purchase a controlling share, fire the management, and appoint new management to operate the firm more profitably, raising its stock price and providing a capital gain for the raiders. Thus, it is argued that the stock market is the main disciplinary device in the stockholder–manager relationship. We have raised some objections to this view earlier.

Japan, at least until the mid-1970s when the stock market was relatively unimportant in corporate finance, appears, however, to have had a quite different way of creating efficient management. Firms were largely financed by bank loans, and stockholders had little say in corporate decisions. Japanese firms are organized in groups called *keiretsu*, each of which is associated with a main bank that is responsible for organizing loan consortia for the firms in its group. The bank is in large part responsible for monitoring the firm's management. The bank even protects its firms from takeovers. A bank has an interest in running a tight ship so that its *keiretsu* is an attractive one for new firms, for only if it disciplines unprofitable firms can it easily arrange loan consortia for its *keiretsu*'s members. The bank as a monitor is also prone to take a longer view of risk taking and innovation than the stock market system, which is too much concerned with short-run profitability.

The analogue of the public–planner agency problem under capitalism is the public–stockholder problem, except neither capitalist property relations nor the culture requires the stockholder to be an agent of the public. At this point, the theory of capitalism invokes Adam Smith: stockholders, that is to say, firm owners, are directed to undertake those actions that are in the public interest as if by an invisible hand. We have already discussed the limitations of this view and the consequent growth of government intervention in all advanced capitalist countries over the past century.

We now introduce our alternative(s) to privatization. They involve (1) the use of competitive markets for allocating the private goods that are allocated by markets in advanced capitalist economies (this may exclude health services and education, a point which is peripheral to our concerns here), (2) the adoption of bank-centric monitoring of firms, much as in Japan or Germany, coupled with a decentralized way of distributing firm profits, which will induce banks to monitor firms properly, while distributing profits in a way that would be far more equal than under capitalism, and (3) political competition (i.e., democracy), whose job will be, inter alia, to set the parameters of government intervention through party competition. We think the principal economic variable with respect to which the government should intervene is the aggregate level and sectoral distribution of investment, for these investment variables are almost certainly non-optimal in market equilibria without intervention due to the absence of a full set of insurance and futures markets. In addition, the government would, of course, retain its functions of providing public goods, antitrust regulation, education and health services, and transfer payments.

We propose two variants, which differ in the mechanism by which profits are distributed. A feasible mechanism for denationalizing firms in an economy that lacks the set of institutions necessary for a stock market to work well is partially modelled after the Japanese combination of *keiretsu* with a main bank, which evolved, indeed, when Japanese financial markets were underdeveloped. The set of firms would be partitioned into groups, each group consisting of firms that are to some extent technologically related and each group being associated with a main bank. Banks would own shares of firms, and each firm in a group would own some shares of the other firms in its group as well. The board of directors of a firm would consist of representatives of the main bank and of the other firms who hold its shares. The bank's profits (including its share of firms' profits in its group) would return in large part to the government, to be spent on public goods, health services, education, and so on: this would constitute one part of a citizen's consumption of aggregate profits. In addition, each firm would receive dividends from its shares of other firms in its group, and these would be distributed to its workers, constituting the second part of a citizen's share of profit income. Because citizens' income would come in part from the profits of other firms in their *keiretsu*, they would have an interest in requiring those firms to maximize profits, an interest that would be looked after by her firm's representatives on the boards of directors of the other firms. Because the ownership of Firm A would be highly concentrated in the main bank and a relatively small number of other firms, call them B, C, and D, it would be worthwhile for each of B, C, and D to expend the costs to monitor Firm A. If Firm A started performing badly, Firms B, C, and D would be able to sell their stock in A to the main bank, which would have an obligation to buy it. This would put pressure on the bank to discipline Firm A's management.

In this scheme, profits would not be distributed exactly equally across the population. Presumably, the share of profits that finances the publicly provided goods would be distributed universally (health services and education), but the share that citizens receive through the portfolio held by the firm in which they work would be unequal, due to the differential profitability of firms. In any case, the distribution of profits would be far more egalitarian than it is in a capitalist economy.

The salient points of this abbreviated description are that (1) banks would monitor firm management and would be induced to do so by (2) pressure from other firms, whose employees' incomes depended in part on the performance of other firms in their group, while (3) firms would be competent to monitor other firms by virtue of their technological relatedness, and the main bank would also develop expertise in that technological sector. The usual difficulty of organizing small, diffuse shareholders of a firm to monitor its management would be overcome because (4) a firm's shareholders, although each individually small, would be concentrated, geographically and industrially, in the workforce of its cousin firms in the *keiretsu*. And (5) total profits in the economy would be distributed in a far more egalitarian fashion than in any actually existing capitalist economy. Finally, a special dispensation (through the tax system) would have to be provided to citizens in the nonprofit sector (e.g., education and health) with an equivalent to the dividend a worker in a *keiretsu* receives as his or her share of profit income.

A variant of denationalization that could be used in an economy with advanced financial institutions and a stock exchange is somewhat different.

The first step would be to distribute vouchers to all adults, giving each a per capita claim on the profits of each firm in the country. More realistically, mutual funds could be set up and the vouchers distributed to adult citizens could be invested in the mutual funds, which would use them, in turn, to purchase shares of firms. If a capitalist stock market were then opened, prices in voucher coupon units would eventually equilibrate for shares of these mutual funds and firms. There would, furthermore, be an equilibrium price of a voucher coupon in terms of money. Thus, while firms would initially be owned entirely by voucher holders, vouchers would be freely tradeable for money. What is quite likely is that most citizens would sell their voucher shares to the rich, exiting the stock market, not only because they would not have had experience with stock markets, but also because of their relatively higher rate of time preference than the rich.

But we propose that the stock market be limited as follows: while citizens would be free to trade their stock in mutual funds for stock in other mutual funds, they could not liquidate their portfolios, that is, turn them into cash. Thus it would not be possible to exchange vouchers for money. Vouchers would provide a claim on the future profit stream of a firm, but that stream could not be capitalized at its present discounted value.

The first virtue of this coupon stock market economy is that it should provide the same disciplinary stimulus to firm managers that a capitalist stock market does. If a firm's management were performing poorly, the mutual funds holding the firm's stock would sell, causing a fall in its coupon stock price. This would be a signal to the banks that the firm was in trouble, and the firm would be hard-pressed to finance its operations. Since vouchers provide no equity for the firm, financing would come from bank loans: a main bank associated with each firm. The board of directors of a firm would be comprised of representatives of the mutual funds that owned it and its main bank.

Would the selling of shares of poorly performing mutual funds by citizens suffice to guarantee their good management? Presumably the salaries of fund managers would be highly sensitive to the performance of the fund and they would quickly unload stock of a poorly performing firm in their portfolio. This would decrease the firm's rating on the bond market, causing its main bank to step in and discipline management, for the bank's reputation and its managers' incomes would depend on the creditworthiness of the firms in its jurisdiction. The incentives for the managers of the main banks to carry out their monitoring task are discussed later.

The second virtue of the coupon economy is that it would prevent the concentration of ownership of firms in the hands of a small class: thus, it would provide, if not a guarantee, then something close to it, that profits of firms would be distributed roughly equally in the population. We assume that the mechanism of requiring citizens to hold shares of mutual funds, and not firms directly, would prevent uninformed individuals from losing their stock assets by making poor investments. Government regulation of the mutual funds would be necessary.

We can think of a number of criticisms of the coupon proposal. By not allowing citizens to capitalize their rights to profit streams from firms, we prevent them from shifting consumption from the future to the present, and hence create Pareto inefficiency. Our response is first that apart from private behavior being sometimes too myopic from the social point of view, there is a negative externality associated with the concentration of shares that would follow if citizens could liquidate their shares: the creation of a small class of large shareholders, with concomitant political power (see later).

It can also be objected that financial markets will find ways of de facto allowing people to capitalize their shares. For example, some firms might pay out their capital stock as dividends. This problem could be addressed by setting a maximum fraction of profits that could be paid out to shareholders. As a way of mitigating this problem, we suggest that citizens be allowed to use their coupon-share assets as collateral with banks for (large) loans. For the period of the loan the bank would manage the borrower's portfolio, deducting the loan payments from the income stream. Another problem would exist with regard to foreign investment. Foreigners would not have access to coupons; their investments in domestic firms must necessarily take the form of real equity. Thus, citizens could invest money in domestic firms through foreign agents. Again, this possibility would require some regulation of foreign investment.

In sum, this variant would also maintain a roughly egalitarian distribution of profits, while taking advantage of what useful features the stock market possesses in providing signals of the effectiveness of firm management.

The major question one must raise with respect to both *keiretsu* and coupon proposals, which depend on the main bank as the primary monitor of the public firms, is who monitors the monitor? If the main bank depends substantially on the state for finance, the political aspect of the soft-budget constraint looms large.

Whenever the benefits of state policies of leniency in underwriting losses, of refinancing, or of providing relief or subsidies are concentrated and highly visible, while the costs of such policies are diffuse, inevitable political pressure on the state builds to follow such policies, whether in a capitalist or a communist country. But such pressure is less resistible in the latter than in the former. In capitalist countries, while large bailouts by the state are not uncommon, the prevailing ideology makes layoffs and bankruptcies politically more tolerable. All systems make costly mistakes from time to time; under bank monitoring (including under our proposed system), what are called Type 2 errors (namely, bad projects are allowed to continue too long) are likely to be more common than Type 1 errors (namely, projects are abandoned too soon) that seem to characterize the harsh, if occasionally myopic, exit mechanisms of capitalist stock market economies. Different societies have different degrees of tolerance for these two types of error. Societies that value stability and security more than mobility and change seem to have a larger degree of tolerance for Type 2 errors.

While it is difficult to escape completely the politics of the soft-budget constraint, we believe that the problem may be less virulent under our proposed insider monitoring system with proper safeguards. We spell out several reasons:

1. In the two variants proposed, between the public firm, which is an independent joint-stock company, and the state treasury, there is a hard layer formed by equity-holding, technologically interdependent affiliate firms (or mutual funds) and a main bank that orchestrates reciprocal monitoring. This layer imposes some financial discipline on public firms and acts as a buffer against direct political accountability. This, of course, is not enough to prevent the whole affiliate group from acting as a lobby with government for a troubled member.

2. The reputational concerns of the main bank's managers may act as an antidote for being susceptible to political pressures. In Japan, even though the banks have been closely regulated by the Ministry of Finance, there is some keenness on the part of the bank managers to preserve their reputations as good monitors, and there is competition among banks in seeking the position of main bank for well-run firms. In our proposed system it would not be difficult to keep track of the reputation of bank managers, since the number of main banks would be relatively small. The managerial labor market does not "forget" if bank managers forgive bad loans of nonperforming firms under their management too often.

3. It is important to introduce incentive features in the payment structures of main bank (as well as mutual fund) managers linked to their performance

of monitoring firms. While the social loss from a bad project may be many times the personal loss to the bank manager's linked income, that personal loss may be a significant enough fraction of his or her income to make negligence rather costly.

4. It is important to keep open the doors of international competition, as a check on the institutional monitors' laxity. International market signals can also provide valuable guidelines and comparative reference points in the main banks' monitoring process and raise cost and quality consciousness all around. There are genuine cases for infant-industry protection, but to prevent the overly common degeneration of infant industries into geriatric protection lobbies, a clearly specified fixed duration should be announced for such protection, after which the firm must sink or swim in international competition. To make such precommitments credible, some binding international trade agreements may be tried.

5. It is often claimed that under the soft-budget constraint, the state remains as the risk absorber of last resort, and so little incentive remains on the part of managers to avoid overly risky projects. Yet in actual cases of public-sector management, one often finds too few, rather than too many, risks taken by managers. This is due largely to too much political accountability: the managers are constantly wary of taking bold decisions that might be seen by their political bosses as rocking the boat of the preexisting patronage distribution system. Even in our proposed system, it may be difficult for the state to credibly precommit not to intervene too often in the main bank's decision-making process. Some difficult-to-change constitutional guarantees of the infrequency of state intervention in the short- to medium-run operations of the banks may be necessary.

6. There should also be, as Sah and Weitzman (1991) have suggested, well-publicized liquidation precommitments for investment projects *before* they are launched, should their cumulative performance at prespecified dates in the future not exceed certain threshold levels. The rescue strategies by the main bank of a corporate group, which we have already indicated, will be subject, by prior legislative enactment, to this kind of liquidation precommitment.

7. Although in our system the state is to own directly a majority of the shares of a main bank, some significant fraction of the shares may be owned by pension funds, insurance companies, and other banks, to allow for some diversification of interest in and professional control of the main bank's lending operations.

We intend the variants of the last subsections to apply to large firms. Small firms could be privately owned. Innovations would take place in the R&D labs of large firms and by entrepreneurs in small firms. A successful small firm that grew would either eventually incorporate, in which case it would become part of the "coupon" sector or join a *keiretsu*, and then it would be eligible for financing from the public banks. Or successful firms might be nationalized upon reaching a given size, with compensation. Most small firms under capitalism either die eventually or are purchased by large firms, and the same trajectory could be expected in our proposed systems.

There are alternative models oriented more than ours to the labor market and the important issues of worker participation and motivation, as opposed to our emphasis on financial systems and managerial motivation. One such model is of an economy consisting of labor-managed firms. This model is not inconsistent with our mechanism of bank-centric monitoring, although it may not achieve the degree of egalitarianism that we find desirable. We can note here that our proposed insider-monitoring system also provides a solution for some of the adverse incentive and agency problems that many critics of labor-managed firms have pointed out: the main bank will monitor and discipline the firm against the possible tendency toward excessive wage payments or myopic capital consumption.

Finally, we address the principal question that motivates our goal of maintaining a roughly egalitarian distribution of firms' profit streams. If equity is our concern, why not distribute ownership of firms equally to all citizens, via vouchers, and then allow a fully liberalized stock market? Versions of this proposal have been under discussion in Poland and the former Czechoslovakia. Granted, this would probably result, quite quickly, in the concentration of firm ownership in the hands of a small class of otherwise rich citizens. But so what? By selling their shares of firms to the rich, average citizens would simply capitalize that asset, and so they would be no worse off (and, perhaps, better off) than had they held on to their shares.

This argument, however, works only under two assumptions: (1) that the vast majority of citizens are wise investors, who have somewhat educated estimates of the future profitability of firms, and (2) that there are no negative externalities to the concentration of firm ownership in the portfolios of a small class. If only (1) fails, then one might simply forbid the trading of shares for money for a short period of time (several years), during which people would become educated about the stock market. But we shall argue that (2) fails as well and that there is, therefore, good reason never to allow the trading of coupons or shares of firms purchased with them for money.

A number of public bads positively affect the profitability and productivity of firms. The obvious example is the amount of pollution firms can emit. The legal levels of these public bads are set, ultimately, by the public through the electoral process, and, we claim, the level that the electoral process will produce depends upon the distribution of profit income among the citizenry. Other examples of such public bads are the logging of primeval forests, or pernicious advertising, such as for cigarettes and alcohol.

At first thought, it might appear that, so long as firms are profit-maximizing, they will put pressure on the electorate to allow high levels of this kind of public bad. This may well be true. What will vary with the distribution of profit income in the economy, however, is the size and wealth of the coalition of citizens who have an economic interest in a large level of public bads. It can be shown that for a large and reasonable class of possible preference orderings, the optimal level of public bads for individuals increases with the share of social profits they receive (Roemer 1991).

How is a particular level of public bads realized in a capitalist society? It is the consequence of private decisions taken by firms and public decisions taken through the political process. Through both of these mechanisms, the preferences of those who receive large shares of corporate profits are disproportionately represented. Obviously this is so for decisions made by the boards of directors of private firms and corporations. It also holds with regard to the political process, because those who own large shares of firms are powerful in lobbying, advertising, influencing or controlling the media and therefore shaping public opinion, as well as in financing electoral campaigns and political parties. It therefore would not be surprising if the level of public bads that is realized in a modern capitalist economy reflects disproportionately the desired level of those who own large shares of firm profits and who, as stated earlier, therefore want high levels of the public bads.

In either the coupon or the *keiretsu* economy, everyone is constrained to receive approximately the same share of total profits. Although there surely would be wealthy citizens, whose wage income and savings were high, there would be no class of citizens whose profit income would be substantially greater than the profit income of others. Hence, no small class of citizens would have an interest in advocating as high a level of public bads as do the wealthy in a capitalist economy.[61]

We do not harbor illusions about the formidable problems, political and economic, of the possible transition to our proposed system. That transition would surely require the development of new institutions, but possibly not many more than, or organizationally more difficult than, those required for the transition to capitalism. In the immediate future both types of transition will involve common and difficult problems: for example, breaking state monopolies, ending large-scale public subsidies, introducing markets and competition along with their inevitable painful readjustments and dislocations, organizing joint-stock companies and a viable commercial banking system, overhauling the legal system. The bank-centric monitoring system may be less difficult to introduce in some developing countries where there is a pre-existing set of public investment banks and financial institutions.

We have claimed that introducing competition, markets, and political democracy are the crucial parts of the reform program, not large-scale privatization. Some of the popular horror stories about inefficient public firms or parastatals in developing or communist countries may have more to do with their being monopolies than with their being publicly owned. There are many examples of efficient public firms in competitive environments around the world. Empirical evidence of significant efficiency differentials between public and private firms after adjusting for market structure (and regulatory policy) is quite scanty. We have argued that, with appropriate institutional restructuring, incentive and efficiency issues can be handled without privatization. One hopes that this point of view will not be summarily dismissed simply because, in the current populist discourse in some of the East European countries, the notion of public ownership brings bad memories of something imposed on them in its name, or because, in the simple-minded ideology of the free-marketeers in those countries and their Western patrons, the market mechanism can function only with full-scale capitalist property rights.

Conclusion

What makes democracies sustainable? And, in turn, what are the principal dangers facing new democracies? These are the questions that motivated our analyses. Our intent was to identify the principal political and economic choices confronting new democracies in the South and the East and to examine these alternatives in the light of our conception of sustainable democracy. While we have presented several proposals, concerning both institutional design and policy orientations, our purpose was not to offer blueprints, but only to emphasize that choices are inevitable and that alternatives are available.

What makes democracies sustainable, given the context of exogenous conditions, are their institutions and performance. Democracy is sustainable when its institutional framework promotes normatively desirable and politically desired objectives, such as freedom from arbitrary violence, material security, equality, or justice, and when, in turn, these institutions are adept at handling crises that arise when such objectives are not being fulfilled.

Institutions have two distinct effects: (1) There are sufficient grounds to believe that the specific institutional arrangements that make up a particular democratic system also affect its performance. Our knowledge of institutions is inadequate: normative arguments are inconclusive and the empirical knowledge of the effects of particular arrangements is limited. Yet the Churchillian view of democracy as the least evil is just not enough. Democracies are not all the same, and what they are matters for how they perform. (2) In turn, the effect of exogenous circumstances on the survival of democracies depends on their particular institutional arrangements. Democratic stability is not just a matter of economic, social, or cultural conditions because specific institutional arrangements differ in their ability to process conflicts, particularly when these conditions become so adverse that democratic performance is experienced as inadequate.

Culturally heterogeneous societies present particularly difficult problems in the design of institutions that would channel conflicts into the framework of a rule-governed interplay of interests. Conflicts between central authorities, intent on preserving territorial integrity, and regional forces, seeking to increase autonomy, are difficult to resolve. Institutional failures at the center induce separatist challenges, and such failures are likely when authoritarian regimes collapse. Civil wars and violations of human rights can, however, be avoided. Peaceful answers can be found in institutional designs that treat cultural conflicts as a matter of politics rather than accept them as primordially real. While the central government has an interest in inhibiting escalating demands for autonomy, it must negotiate with democratically elected representatives from regions that seek it. The experience of several countries shows that mutually acceptable compromises are possible if an institutional framework is established early, if this framework is sufficiently flexible to leave the resolution of particular conflicts to the political process and if it is at the same time sufficiently rigid to prevent escalations of demands. Thus, while democracy in multicultural societies must necessarily have different institutional arrangements, sustainable democracy is feasible under the conditions of cultural pluralism.

The fact that, under democracy, rulers are repeatedly elected provides both incentives for governments to be responsive to the wishes of majorities (Manin 1995) and for the temporary losers to continue to channel their demands within the framework of the competitive institutions (Przeworski 1991).

The conditions under which democratic institutions generate incentives for governments to be accountable are quite stringent; they are not met by all institutional frameworks. Governments are accountable only when voters can clearly assign the responsibility for performance to competing teams of politicians, when the incumbents can be effectively punished for inadequate performance in office, and when voters are sufficiently well informed to accurately assess this performance. Moreover, to return to Shugart and Carey (1992), the electoral "efficiciency" that favors accountability can be achieved only at some cost of representation of diverse interests and, as studies of the determinants of voter turnout indicate, of electoral participation.

Heeding Rousseau's warning that the effects of institutions depend on specific social and cultural conditions, we hesitate to follow those who offer a blueprint for an optimal democratic system. Imitation of any of the institutional frameworks that have passed the test of time in the established democracies – and these frameworks differ in significant ways – seems particularly risky if we believe, as we found grounds at least to suspect, that many of the conditions that have sustained the established democracies are absent in the countries that have only recently experienced a process of democratic transition.

Indeed, even if were able to identify the optimal institutions, there is no reason to think that the political forces in conflict over the institutional design would end up choosing them. Institutions affect not only efficiency but also distribution, and are thus inevitably subject to conflict. And, as in many strategic situations, partisan and collective rationality are likely to diverge: the institutional framework that results from such conflicts need not be the most effective or enduring one under the specific historical conditions.

Moreover, conflicts over institutions tend to be protracted. While transitions to democracy entail by definition a transformation of the institutional system, in particular free elections, they do not necessarily cause changes in the relation of political forces, policy orientations, or the economic and social patterns. And since such changes are typically expected by the forces struggling against the ancien régime, disenchantment with the transformations achieved thus far is a characteristic phenomenon in the early stages of a new democracy. Political forces tend to divide between those who maintain that the necessary transformations have been achieved and those who want to go further, often in divergent directions.

Democracy is sustained when all major political forces find it best to pursue their interests and values within the institutional framework. And this means not only that these institutions must offer channels for the representation of diverse interests, but that participation must make a difference for the welfare of the eventual participants. Yet most recent transitions to democracy have coincided with an inherited economic crisis. Moreover, the very economic reforms that are necessary to resume growth tend to engender at least temporarily an additional decline in consumption by large segments of the population. Hence, most new democracies face the challenge of having to consolidate the nascent political institutions when material conditions continue to deteriorate. This is the central dilemma facing most new democracies.

Searching for a solution to this dilemma, we argued that stabilization and liberalization are not sufficient to generate growth unless these reforms are targeted to redress the fiscal crisis and to mobilize public savings, that a reform of the public sector rather than mass privatization better combines efficiency and equality, that without a social protection net political conditions for the continuation of reforms become eroded, and that a technocratic style of policy making weakens the nascent democratic institutions. These arguments lead to some prescriptive consequences, namely, that a social protection net should be installed when reforms are launched, that the entire reform package must minimize the transitional social costs and must be designed with a view toward resumed growth, and, finally, that reform programs should be formulated and implemented as a result of a political interplay of representative organizations within the framework of the representative institutions. These recommendations are not intended as a recipe: we are far from certain to what extent they are feasible and whether they are sufficient. The issues entailed in the interplay of democratic and economic reforms are so difficult that they cannot be resolved by any magic recipes. We do believe, however, that several trade-offs – notably between stabilization and growth, between social expenditures and growth, between social expenditures and the sustainability of reforms, and between political participation and the sustainability of reforms – are misconceived within the model that underlies the currently fashionable policy prescriptions.

What then are the main dangers facing the new democracies? The traditional fear in Latin America has been the restoration of a military dictatorship. Civilian authoritarian governments, based on an amalgam of nationalist and religious ideologies, are a more credible threat in Eastern Europe. But perhaps the most acute danger is one of social disintegration. If the economic crisis continues and if the state is further weakened, to the point of not being able to enforce rights and obligations predictably, decentralized collective violence might then ensue.

Hence, we return to where we began: the state. Repeatedly, we have been sounding an alarm at the prospect of a further weakening of state institutions. Indeed, we have become convinced in the course of these analyses that several of the dangers facing new democratic regimes are due to the inability of state institutions to guarantee physical security, to establish conditions for an effective exercise of citizenship, to provide moral leadership, to mobilize public savings, to coordinate resource allocation, and to correct income distribution. The principal mistake of neoliberal prescriptions is that they underestimate the role of state institutions in organizing both the public and the private life of groups and individuals. Without an effective state, there can be no democracy.

If we believe that the state has an economic, besides a political role to play, why are we in favor of market-oriented reforms? We see stabilization, principally a reduction of the fiscal crisis with all its attendant consequences, as inevitable once an economy enters an inflationary spiral. Moreover, we recognize that an increased reliance on markets, national and international, to allocate resources is required to enhance efficiency in economies that are monopolistic, overregulated, and overprotected. Competitive markets are necessary to achieve an efficient and vigorous economy. Yet we do not think that the remedy consists of weakening the state. We challenged both the view that economic growth can be resumed in the absence of state intervention and the view that full-scale private ownership is indispensable for an efficient use of productive assets.

Economic strategies have political consequences. First, the rapid internationalization of economic and political relations requires national governments to alienate some traditional instruments of economic policy. This reduced sovereignty, in turn, restricts the scope of decisions controlled by the democratic process. Collective choices are so constrained that little appears at stake in political participation. This is perhaps one reason why organizational life is anemic, not only in the new but also in the established democracies. Second, the technocratic policy style, characteristic of the pro-market reforms, tends to undermine the nascent representative institutions. Finally, indiscriminate cuts of public expenditures reduce the very capacity of the state to guarantee the effective exercise of citizenship rights, particularly in the areas of police protection, education, and income maintenance. Pushed to the extreme, they threaten the very integrity of the state.

The danger of collective violence is not limited to those countries that face challenges to their territorial integrity. They are also caused by political, educational, and social inequalities that exclude large segments of the population from the effective exercise of the rights and obligations of citizenship. Even if democracy is the regime where all subjects become citizens, only an effective state can generate the conditions that ensure the realization of citizenship. Citizenship can be implemented only when the normative system is guided by universal criteria, when the rule of law is effectively enforced, and when public powers are willing and able to protect rights and obligations. Yet many new democracies face multiple challenges of providing an effective citizenship under economic and institutional conditions that undermine the viability of state institutions. The result is that states are incapable of uniformly enforcing standardized bundles of rights and obligations. We thus face the specter of democratic political regimes without effective citizenship in large geographic areas or for significant social sectors.

This specter is foreboding. The state is crucial in constituting social order, in enabling regular and peaceful private relations among groups and individuals. If state institutions are unable to enforce rights and obligations in large geographic areas or for significant social sectors, private interactions lose their predictable character. When the state is reduced to the point that it cannot provide physical protection and access to basic social services, public order collapses: material survival and even physical safety can be only privately secured. Private systems of violence are then likely to emerge; violence is likely to become decentralized, anomic, and widespread. Under such conditions, it is not only democracy that is threatened, but the very bases of social cohesion.

Notes

1. It is amusing to note that this same sentence read in the proposal for this project, written in early 1989: "And contrary to dire predictions, this list will soon extend to Eastern European countries. Even in the Soviet Union, the first timid opening met with a massive expression of popular will and forced democracy on the political agenda."

2. According to *The Guardian* (30 April 1991), "A steering group of the larger industrial economies [G10] yesterday called on the new democracies of eastern Europe to abandon 'gradualism' and adopt the Polish model of rapid economic reforms." According to Reuter (6 June 1991), finance, trade and foreign ministers of the OECD countries hoped "that the USSR and the Republics would move quickly to introduce the broad range of . . . reforms necessary to move to a market economy." In the words of the OECD statement "Transition from the Command to a Market Economy" (1990: 9), "While a gradualist approach may cause lesser social tensions, a long period of moderate reforms entails the danger that both reformers and the population will 'become tired of reforms,' as they do not seem to bring visible changes. Also during a long period of reforms various anti-reform and other lobbies may mobilize their forces and may gradually strangle the reform process." As Nelson (1984: 108) observed, "Advocates of 'shock treatment' are convinced that public tolerance for sacrifice is brief and that the courage of politicians is likewise limited. If the adjustment process is too gradual, opposition will gather and the process will be derailed."

   Moreover, this urging to rush is not just a matter of advice. As Michael H. Wilson, Canada's minister for international trade commented after an OECD meeting, "It has been made pretty clear by a number of countries that until there has been a substantial demonstration of the will to take those decisions on reform and their actual implementation, there simply is not the money available" (*International Herald Tribune*, 6 June 1991). And, indeed, the Polish government interpreted the 50 percent debt reduction granted to Poland by the Paris Club as "a compensation for courage" demonstrated by the country in its pursuit of market economy (Janusz Lewandowski, Minister of Privatization, *Liberation*, 16 March 1991).

3. Note, however, Asselain's (1984) argument that in Eastern Europe the planning system became complex independently of the complexity of the economy.

4. See several tables in *Polacy 88: Dynamika konflikty a szansy reform* and Przeworski (1993a).

5. Here are some Polish expressions of this strategy. (The italics are ours.) In his inaugural speech to the Sejm, the first postcommunist prime minister, Tadeusz Mazowiecki, announced that "the government will undertake steps initiating the transition to *modern market economy, tested by the experience of developed coun-*

tries'' (Domarańczyk, 1990: 148). Speaking to the annual meeting of the IMF and the World Bank in September 1989, Leszek Balcerowicz, deputy prime minister and minister of finance, announced the government's intention ''to transform the Polish economy into *a market economy, with the ownership structure changing in the direction of that found in the advanced industrial economies''* (*Financial Times*, 16 July 1990). According to Marcin Swiecicki, minister of economic cooperation, ''In reforming our economy, we do not seek experiments. We do not want our economists to invent new systems but that they adopt *solutions that work elsewhere. We simply want to construct a market economy like in the West''* (*Liberation*, 14 February 1990: 32). As Sadowski, Iwanek, and Najdek (1990: 1) observed, ''It is the declared objective of the present government of Poland to build *a market economy modelled after the Western developed market economies.''*

6. This strategy was developed in fact in the late 1980s by the BNDES (Banco Nacional de Desenvolvimento Econômico e Social).

7. Eastern Europe may appear to contradict this observation. The Soviet Union did attempt to impose its political institutions and economic integration on the Eastern European countries. Yet the model of economic development was to a large extend autarkic: note that even the Stalinist conception of development produced large steel mills in each country. And to the extent to which this model was internationalist, it turned out to be unworkable precisely because it hurled itself against national aspirations.

8. Clearly, national sovereignty was restricted in the political, economic, and cultural realm by the Soviet domination of Eastern Europe. What is new about the strategy of modernization by internationalization is that this sovereignty is being, at least in part, surrendered voluntarily, although under the pressure of economic conditions.

9. It seems incredible today that only some ten years ago, the French Socialist Party won an electoral majority under the slogan *''Changer la Vie.''* The past president of the European Bank for Reconstruction, the author of that program, was proposing that the government should establish popular ateliers, where he would himself repair his car rather than pay specialized workers to do it.

10. These are democracies that by 1989 had a per capita income of at least 5,000 1985 U.S. dollars expressed in purchasing power parity equivalents (PPP USD) and that in 1951 had an income of less than 2,500 1985 PPP USD. Note that this is a permissive definition of ''the First World'': 5,000 USD is only 27 percent of per capita income in the United States in 1988. Mexico had an income of 4,999 USD in 1988 (2,378 USD in 1951) and Taiwan of 5,708 USD (677 USD in 1951), and both are at the threshold of democracy.

11. One might expect that this strategy also mitigates the costs of modernization by increasing the flow of foreign aid to countries that adopt it. Yet, in 1991 the total flow of foreign assistance to the less developed countries amounted to $133.4 billion, while capital outflows due to debt servicing reached $141 billion. Moreover, the cost to the less developed countries of import restrictions by the more developed countries is estimated to be in excess of $150 billion.

12. For a recent summary of these results, see World Bank (1992).

13. Intercountry inequality is a more important source of worldwide individual inequality than is intracountry inequality (Summers, Kravis, and Heston 1984; Berry, Bourguignon, and Morrison 1991). Not without some heroic assumptions, Berry, Bourguignon, and Morrison (1991) examined the distribution of income at the world scale. They concluded (p. 75) that among nonsocialist countries "for 1950–86 there was an unambiguous worsening of income distribution. The top two deciles gained, albeit not dramatically, the next decile's share was unchanged and each of the bottom deciles lost, especially those in the middle (fourth to seventh). The share of the bottom seven deciles fell from 17.7 percent to 15.3 percent. . . . For the middle deciles, especially the seventh and eighth the marked gains of the 1950s and 1960s were canceled out by the losses of the 1970s and (especially) the 1980s." They also found that intercountry differences contribute more to global inequality than do internal differences.

A comparison of national data collected by Fields (1988: Table 15.1) with the *World Development Report 1992* (World Bank 1992), shows that between circa 1970 and the most recent date available, typically mid-1980s, the income share of the bottom 40 percent of households increased in India, the Philippines, and Spain, was more or less unchanged in Brazil, the United States, and Japan, and declined in Pakistan, Sri Lanka, Costa Rica, and Yugoslavia. Boron (1991) showed a dramatic increase of inequality in Argentina during the 1980s, while Cortés and Rubalcava (1992) found that income inequality increased in Mexico between 1984 and 1989.

The functional distribution of income shows an unambiguous and dramatic worldwide trend in favor of incomes from property. Comparisons of data provided by the World Bank show that the share of labor in the value added in manufacturing declined dramatically in almost all countries, more and less developed.

14. Posing the question in this way does not assume that new democracies are less capable of managing economic crises than are established democracies or authoritarian regimes. According to some arguments, the capacity of new democracies to undertake stabilization programs and to implement structural reforms is hampered by the vast expectations of economic improvements they generate and by their vulnerability to popular pressures and to interest-group influence, while electoral cycles and pluralist competition undermine their ability for long-term planning (Ames 1987; Stallings and Kaufman 1989; Marer 1991). Yet new democracies appear to have been no less able to impose economic discipline in hard times. Comparative studies of economic reforms in the less developed countries have shown no systematic differences among regimes in the choice of economic reform strategies (Nelson 1990) and in economic performance (Remmer 1986, 1990; Haggard et al. 1990). And even if it were true that authoritarian regimes are more capable of imposing and persevering with economic reforms, we would not be willing to treat democracy as an instrumental value, to be judged by its consequences for economic performance. The question we pose is not how regimes affect the success of economic reforms, but whether there are ways to resume growth under democratic conditions.

15. All the subsequent figures are expressed in 1985 PPP USD.

16. Bruszt and Simon (1991) asked respondents in nine countries whether they prefer

a system in which (1) owners manage the firm or appoint managers, (2) owners and employers jointly appoint managers, (3) the state owns and appoints managers, and (4) employees own and appoint managers. The last alternative was most popular in Bulgaria, Lithuania, Rumania, Slovenia, and Ukraine; it came second in Hungary and Poland, in both cases after comanagement.

17. The classic statement is Benedict Anderson, *Imagined Communities* (1983). That Peruvian creoles could in the early nineteenth century identify themselves as sharing a nation with Guaranis but not with Spaniards is telling proof for Anderson that a nation cannot be defined by objective conditions. Even Karl Deutsch's criteria (in *Nationalism and Social Communication,* 1953), that of high levels of communication in ratio to the total amount of communication, cannot account for the construction of a Peruvian nation.

18. This argument parallels that of Stanley Lieberson with Lynn Hansen (1974).

19. See David Laitin's (1987) critique of the application of the consociation model to South Africa.

20. In the 1920s, Radical Republican Party elites in Madrid did ally with an anti-Catalanist populist who won many votes for their party from immigrant workers. But the longer-term effect of this strategy was to facilitate a Catalanist coalition that was able to present a far more united front against Madrid than would have been possible without the Radical Republican intervention.

21. Nationality is not then established ex ante. Once a group is mobilized in the name of cultural distinctiveness, no matter how similar or different its people are from those of the center, it will make claims for national autonomy. It serves no analytic purpose to decide whether such claims are historically or culturally reasonable.

22. This point is due to Roger Petersen.

23. Note that this distinction between citizenship rights and the conditions required to make them effective is not the same as the Marxist language of "formal" versus "real" democracy. The latter was based on the argument that in societies that are unequal socially or economically, universal democracy in the political realm only reproduces inequality in the social realm. Our distinction, in turn, is based on the assumption that citizenship can be exercised to alter the inequality in the social realm but only when the social conditions necessary to exercise it are available to all.

24. Even though the counterargument is that if the military are punished and if the armed forces take power again, they will be less likely to release power in the future.

25. Note that in Argentina there was no criminal legislation directed specifically at the kind of crimes that were perpetuated by the military, no established standards of evidence, and no bureaucratic units charged with pursuing violations of rights (Moreno Ocampo 1991).

26. On this topic, see the essays in Elster and Slagstad (1988).

27. The United States is an obvious case that goes against this hypothesis: it is a stable democratic system with highly limited access to politics and horrendous social exclusion.

28. For a summary of such conceptions, see Stepan (1978: chap. 1).

29. We use the past tense because centralized collective bargaining collapsed in Sweden in the early 1980s, while social democratic parties were voted out of office in Sweden and Norway. Hence, the "social democratic model" no longer functioned in the 1980s. Whether the reasons for this demise were inherent in the model or external to it is a matter of controversy. See Moene and Wallerstein (1992) and Przeworski (1993c).

30. Among the seven countries compared in the most careful research on this topic to date, the segment of the population who were poor after taxes and transfers in the mid-1980s was 4.8 percent (195,000) in Norway, 5.0 percent (410,000) in Sweden, 6.0 percent (3.23 million) in West Germany, 8.8 percent (1.61 million) in the United Kingdom, 12.1 percent (2.88 million) in Canada, 14.5 percent (446,000) in Israel, and 16.9 percent (36.88 million) in the United States (Rainwater, Torrey, and Smeeding 1989).

31. It would take us to far from our universe of countries to inquire whether the social and political conditions in the new democracies are in fact distinct from those we assume to be present in the stable democracies. Note that at least the lament about the weakness of political parties seems almost as old as representative democracy itself. On the relation between democracy and representation see Manin (1995).

32. The estimates of the impact of the collapse of the CMEA trade on Eastern European trade vary somewhat, but they indicate that this collapse is responsible for between one-third and one-half of the loss of GDP. For the estimates, see Bruno (1993), Rodrik (1992), Rosati (1993).

33. For arguments that market-oriented reforms necessarily cause a transitional decline of consumption see Przeworski (1991, chap. 4) and Blanchard et al. (1991: 10–11). Argentina seems to be the only country in which output and consumption did not decline as a result of stabilization, but this is an extreme case since the last stabilization program followed a severe and long-lasting decline of output.

34. Except Eastern Europe and South Korea, all the data cited here are derived from articles in Bruno et al. (1991). For Korea, see Rhee (1987). For Eastern Europe, see Przeworski (1992a).

35. The exact figures are disputed; see Morales (1991).

36. Note that Edwards and Edwards (1991: 215) attribute the resumption of growth in Chile after 1985 to increased public investment.

37. One should remember, however, that some significant part of this decline is due to the collapse of the Soviet market, which used to absorb about one-third of the exports from the Eastern European countries.

38. On the static bias of the neoclassical theory, see Fanelli, Frenkel, and Rozenwurcel (1990).

39. This estimate is clearly overoptimistic with regard to Eastern Europe, where there is no labor market to speak of. There is no labor market because there is no housing market, and there is no housing market because housing stock is insufficient and there is no credit market.

40. For example, Jeffrey Sachs, interviewed in Le Figaro (5 December 1990), argued that "from the moment when economic reforms introduced are good (and I believe they are), there is theoretically no reason why they (countries) would not

succeed in their transition. . . . There is real danger of populism or demagogy, which can only impede the reforms."

41. The regression coefficient of percent unemployed in equations explaining the support for the Polish economic program ("the Balcerowicz plan") is about −4.5: for every person unemployed, three and a half others turn against the reform program (Przeworski 1993b).

42. Edwards (1990) seems to be the only person who emphasizes the importance of active labor market policy as an intrinsic element of a reform package, arguing that labor market institutions should be created before stabilization-liberalization.

43. It is worth noting that the increases in unemployment that invariably accompany market-oriented reforms are not necessarily accompanied by a fall in real wages of those who continue to be employed. Wage rates in the private sector rose sharply after stabilization in Great Britain under Thatcher, in Spain, in Bolivia after 1985, and in Chile after 1975, while in all these countries the rate of unemployment hovered in double digits. Only in Eastern Europe did wage rates fall sharply as the economies stabilized. This is a puzzling phenomenon: see the discussion of Bolivia in Bruno et al. (1991). One explanation is that stabilization followed a drastic fall of wages, another one is that the exchange rate was overvalued, and the third is that unemployment had a highly structural character.

44. Morales (1991: 29) presents evidence for Bolivia, Przeworski (1993a) for Poland, and Stokes (1993) for Peru.

45. Grassi (1991) found that among eighteen new democracies, wage militancy is negatively related to government spending, while it has no relation either to unemployment or investment. Hence, it seems that workers are willing to trade social spending for private wages.

46. Note that we are not arguing that the mere presence of unemployment will cause people to turn against the reforms and the governments that pursue them, but only that this will occur if the unemployed have few prospects of finding another job and no income security. In Spain, for example, 58 percent of employed workers voted for the PSOE in the elections of 1986, and so did 57 percent of the unemployed (Feldman, Menes, and Garcia Pardo 1989).

47. According to Sabino (1991: 134), Zelia Cardoso, the former Brazilian minister of finance, decided in the following way the amount of capital levy that constituted the most daring component of the Collor plan:

> While the party continued below, Zelia and her collaborators, in a different room, exchanging ideas and eating sandwiches, were still adding last touches to the plan. From the beginning they disagreed about the maximum level of withdrawals from savings accounts to be permitted: Twenty thousand? Fifty? Seventy? She, as the Minister, would say the final word.
>
> From time to time, to clear her head, she would go down and participate in the party. . . . She wrote on a piece of paper numbers 20, 50 and 70 and returned to the party. She let herself be photographed with some friends, always keeping the piece of paper. Returning to the meeting room, she had decided for fifty thousand cruzeiros. She found the group still discussing the plan.

48. Lechner (1985) and Przeworski (1991) discussed other reasons why concertation with extraparliamentary actors is not a feasible option in the less developed countries.

49. More generally, recent statistical evidence demonstrates that growth is faster in countries which enjoy a more equal distribution of income. The *World Development Report 1991* (World Bank 1991: 137) presents startling data to this effect, while Persson and Tabellini (1991) offer regression analyses for two distinct periods.

50. Saunders and Klau (1985) did not find any effects for the OECD countries, but Swank (1992) did. Blejer and Cheasty (1989) did not find it for the less developed countries.

51. For microevidence, based on interviews with Argentine businessmen, see Lopez (1991).

52. Having examined the characteristics of financial markets in most developing countries, Blejer and Cheasty (1989) concluded that they do not efficiently allocate investments. They cite three reasons: (1) the capital market is undiversified and fragmented; (2) financial returns to savings and/or investment are insufficient; and (3) financial assets bear uncompensated risks.

53. Poznański (1991: 3): "The major lesson from the communist project is not only that this particular model cannot work, but that any attempt at social engineering, even well directed, has to fail, at a very high cost. Such a warning has been coming for years from Hayek (1988), arguing that markets rather than states are the best vehicle not only for the allocation of resources but also for institution building."

54. The Polish minister of industry, Tadeusz Syryjczyk, succinctly stated: "What can be said to the argument that an enterprise belongs to its workers? That farmers, who through a long period carried the burden of industrialization, do not now have any right to national capital? And teachers and doctors? That a young man who works in a factory for one year has a greater right to shares than a pensioner who worked in the same factory for 30 years. If this idea were put into practice, workers of rich enterprises would acquire huge capital, and others nothing." Quoted in Baczyński (1990:7).

55. Akerlof (1970) developed the "lemons principle" for the used car market, which marked the beginning of modern economics of information. The upshot of the principle is that under the condition of asymmetric information between the sellers and the buyers, there may be the case that at no price will any trade take place at all.

56. The Hungarian prime minister, Josef Antall, complained that privatization had generated only 11 billion forint for Hungary in 1990, but government subsidies in the 1991 budget were still as high as 240 billion forint (see *Report on Eastern Europe*, February 1, 1991).

57. Maybe this concern with revenue loss explains the following fact: the State Property Agency in Hungary announced its "first privatization package" in September 1991 to privatize twenty "good" state-owned enterprises, but by September 1991, none of these enterprises had finished the complicated process of valuation and auction (see *Report on Eastern Europe*, October 25, 1991).

58. Indeed, only five state enterprises were sold in 1990 in Poland. The advertising campaign for the public offering of shares of these five firms was designed by a French advertising agency (which charged over a million dollars) (see *European Economy*, special issue, no. 2., 1991: 144).

59. Many Western advisors endorsed this strategy. See Lipton and Sachs (1990) and Blanchard et al. (1991).

60. In the United States, there is a two-tiered structure of lenders of last resort:''The Federal Reserve System is the lender of last resort to member banks and giant member banks are lenders of last resort to institutions and organizations that use the commercial-paper market. This two-tier structure is formalized in the practice requiring units that sell commercial paper to have open lines of credit at commercial banks at least as large as their outstanding commercial paper.'' See Minsky (1986: 50).

61. Indeed, simulations have been run to compare the welfare consequences of an economy where shares are initially equally distributed to citizens and then traded on a fully liberalized stock market with an economy in which shares are initially equally distributed but then traded only in a coupon stock market. Because of the presence of a public bad in production, the majority of the population end up with higher welfare in the coupon economy than in the fully liberalized economy (Roemer 1991).

References

Acuña, Carlos, and Catalina Smulovitz. 1994. "Adjusting the Armed Forces to Democracy: Successes, Failures, and Ambiguities of the Southern Cone Experiences." Unpublished manuscript, Buenos Aires, CEDES.

Akerlof, George. 1970. "The Market for 'Lemons.'" *Quarterly Journal of Economics* 86: 488–500.

Akerlof, George. 1991. "East Germany in from the Cold: The Economic Aftermath of Currency Union." *Brookings Papers on Economic Activity 1:* 1–87.

Alaminos, Antonio. 1991. *Chile: transición política y sociedad.* Madrid: Centro de Investigaciones Sociologicas, Siglo Veintiuno de España.

Alesina, Alberto. 1988. "Macroeconomics and Politics." In *NBER Macroeconomics Annual.* Cambridge, Mass.: MIT Press.

Alesina, Alberto, and Allan Drazen. 1991. "Why Are Stabilizations Delayed?" *American Economic Review 81:* 1175–1188.

Ames, Barry. 1987. *Political Survival: Politicians and Public Policy in Latin America.* Berkeley: University of California Press.

Amsden, Alice H. 1989. *Asia's Next Giant: South Korea and Late Industrialization.* New York: Oxford University Press.

Anderson, Benedict. 1983. *Imagined Communities: Reflections on the Origin and Spread of Nationalism.* New York: Verso.

Aoki. M. 1988. *Information, Incentives, and Bargaining in the Japanese Economy.* Cambridge: Cambridge University Press.

Asselain, Jean-Charles. 1984. *Planning and Profits in a Socialist Economy.* London: Routledge and Kegan Paul.

Baczyński, Jerzy. 1990. "Dla ubogich." *Polityka* (Warsaw). March 3.

Bardhan, Pranab. 1988. "Comment on Gustav Ranis' and John C. H. Fei's 'Development Economics: What Next?'" In Gustav Ranis and T. Paul Schultz, eds., *The State of Development Economics: Progress and Perspectives* (pp. 137–138). Oxford: Basil Blackwell.

Bardhan, Pranab. 1990. "Symposium on the State and Economic Development." *Journal of Economic Perspectives 4:* 3–9.

Bardhan, Pranab, and John Roemer. 1992. "Market Socialism: A Case for Rejuvenation." *Journal of Economic Perspectives 6:* 101–116.

Barro, Robert J. 1989. "A Cross-Country Study of Growth, Saving, and Government." National Bureau of Economic Research Working Paper No. 2855.

Barro, Robert J. 1990. "Government Spending in a Simple Model of Endogenous Growth." *Journal of Political Economy 98:* S103–S125.

Barro, Robert J. 1991. "Economic Growth in a Cross Section of Countries." *Quarterly Journal of Economics 106:* 407–443.

Bates, Robert. 1983. "Modernization, Ethnic Competition, and the Rationality of

Politics in Contemporary Africa.'' In Donald Rothchild and Victor Olorunsola, eds., *State versus Ethnic Claims: African Policy Dilemmas* (pp. 152–171). Boulder: Westview.

Becker, Gary S., Kevin M. Murphy, and Robert Tamura. 1990. ''Human Capital, Fertility, and Economic Growth.'' *Journal of Political Economy 98:* 12–38.

Berglof, E. 1989. ''Capital Structure as a Mechanism of Control: A Comparison of Financial Systems.'' In M. Aoki, B. Gustafsson, and O. E. Williamson, eds., *The Firm as a Nexus of Treaties* (pp. 237–262). London: Sage.

Berry, Albert, Francois Bourguignon, and Christian Morrison. 1991. ''Global Economic Inequality and Its Trends since 1950.'' In Lars Osberg, ed., *Economic Inequality and Poverty. International Perspectives* (pp. 60–91). Armonk, N.Y.: Sharpe.

Blais, Andre, and R. K. Carty. 1988. ''The Effectiveness of Plurality Rule.'' *European Journal of Political Research 18:* 550–553.

Blais, Andre, and R. K. Carty. 1990. ''Does Proportional Representation Foster Voter Turnout?'' *European Journal of Political Research 18:* 167–181.

Blanchard, Oliver, Rudiger Dornbusch, Paul Krugman, Richard Layard, and Lawrence Summers. 1991. *Reform in Eastern Europe.* Cambridge, Mass.: MIT Press.

Blejer, Mario I., and Adrienne Cheasty. 1989. ''Fiscal Policy and Mobilization of Savings for Growth.'' In Mario I. Blejer and Ke-young Chu, eds., *Fiscal Policy, Stabilization, and Growth in Developing Countries* (pp. 33–49). Washington, D.C.: IMF.

Boron, Atilio A. 1991. ''La pobreza de las naciones. La economia politica del neoliberalismo en la Argentina.'' Unpublished manuscript. EURAL, Buenos Aires.

Brada, Josef C., and Arthur E. King. 1992. ''Is There a J-Curve for the Economic Transition from Socialism to Capitalism?'' *Economics of Planning 25:* 37–53.

Bresser Pereira, Luiz Carlos. 1993. ''Economic Reforms and Economic Growth: Efficiency and Politics in Latin America.'' In Luiz Carlos Bresser Pereira, José María Maravall, and Adam Przeworski, *Economic Reforms in New Democracies: A Social-Democratic Approach* (pp. 15–76). Cambridge: Cambridge University Press.

Bruno, Michael. 1991. ''Introduction and Overview.'' In M. Bruno, S. Fischer, E. Helpman, N. Liviatan, and L. Meridor, eds., *Lessons of Economic Stabilization and Its Aftermath* (pp. 1–14). Cambridge, Mass.: MIT Press.

Bruno, Michael. 1993. ''Stabilization and Reform in Eastern Europe: Preliminary Evaluation.'' In Mario I. Blejer, Guillermo Calvo, Fabrizio Corcelli, and Alan H. Gelb, eds., *Eastern Europe in Transition: From Recession to Growth?* World Bank Discussion Paper No. 196. Washington, D.C.: World Bank.

Bruno, M., S. Fischer, E. Helpman, N. Liviatan, and L. Meridor, eds. 1991. *Lessons of Economic Stabilization and Its Aftermath.* Cambridge, Mass.: The MIT Press.

Bruszt, László. 1989. ''The Dilemmas of Economic Transformation in Hungary.'' *Südost Europa 38:* 716–729.

Bruszt, László, and János Simon. 1991. ''Political Culture, Political and Economical Orientations in Central and Eastern Europe during the Transition to Democracy.'' Unpublished manuscript. Erasmus Foundation for Democracy, Budapest.

Budge, Ian, Michael J. Laver, and Kaare Strom. 1994. ''Constraints on Cabinet Formation in Parliamentary Democracies." *American Journal of Political Science 38:* 303–335.

Calvo, Guillermo A. 1989. "Incredible Reforms." In Guillermo Calvo, Ronald Findley, Pentti Kouri and Jorge Braga de Macedo, eds., *Debt, Stabilization and Development: Essays in Memory of Carlos Diaz- Alejandro* (pp. 217–234). London: Basil Blackwell.

CBOS (Centrum Badania Opinii Społecznej). Various issues. *Serwis Informacyjny.* Warsaw.

Cheibub, José Antonio. 1994. Political Regimes, Taxation and Economic Growth: A Comparative Analysis. Ph.D. Dissertation, Department of Political Science, University of Chicago.

Choi, Jang Jip. 1991. "The Façade and Reality of New Democracy in South Korea and Taiwan." East–South Systems Transformations, University of Chicago, Working Paper No. 17.

Comisso, Ellen. 1988. "Market Failures and Market Socialism: Economic Problems of the Transition." *Eastern European Politics and Societies 2:* 433–465.

Comisso, Ellen. 1989. "Crisis in Socialism or Crisis of Socialism? A Review Essay." *World Politics 42:* 563–606.

Comisso, Ellen, Steve Dubb, and Judy McTigue. 1991. "The Illusion of Populism in Latin America and Eastern Europe." East–South Systems Transformations, University of Chicago, Working Paper No.13.

Cortés, Fernando, and Rosa Maria Rubalcava. 1992. "Cambio estructural y concentración: un analisis de la distribución del ingreso familiar en Mexico, 1984–1989." Unpublished manuscript, El Colegio de Mexico.

Cukierman, Alex, Steven B. Webb, and Bilin Neyapti. 1992. "Measuring the Independence of Central Banks and Its Effects on Policy Outcomes." *World Bank Economic Review 6:* 353–398.

Dahl, Robert. 1971. *Polyarchy.* New Haven, Conn.: Yale University Press.

Delich, Francisco. 1984. "Estado, sociedad y fuerzas armadas en la transición argentina." In Augusto Varas, ed., *Transición a la democracia.* Santiago: Asociación Chilena de Investigaciónes para la Paz.

Demoscopia S.A. 1992. Barómetro de Primavera, 1992. In *El País*, April 5.

Deutsch, Karl. 1953. *Nationalism and Social Communication: An Inquiry into the Foundations of Nationality.* New York: Chapman and Hall; Wiley.

Diamond, Larry. 1992. "Economic Development and Democracy Reconsidered." In Gary Marks and Larry Diamond, eds., *Reexamining Democracy: Essays in Honor of Seymour Martin Lipset.* Newbury Park: Sage Publications.

Di Tella, Torcuato. 1991. "Transitions to Democracy in Latin America." East–South Systems Transformations, University of Chicago, Working Paper No. 11.

Dmowski, Roman. 1989. *Myśli Nowoczesnego Polaka.* Warsaw: Wydawnictwo Grunwald.

Domański, H., A. Firkowska-Mankiewicz, K. Janicka, and A. Titkow. 1993. "Społeczeństwo bez reguł." In Andrzej Rychard and Michał Fedorowicz, eds., *Społeczeństwo w transformacji* (pp. 143–169). Warsaw: IFiS PAN.

Domarańczyk, Zbigniew. 1990. *100 dni Mazowieckiego.* Warsaw: Wydawnictwo Andrzej Bonarski.

Dudley, Billy J. 1982. *An Introduction to Nigerian Government and Politics.* Bloomington, Ind.: Indiana University Press.

Eckstein, Harry. 1966. *Division and Cohesion in Democracy.* Princeton, N.J.: Princeton University Press.

Edwards, Sebastian. 1990. "The Sequencing of Economic Reform: Analytical Issues and Lessons from Latin American Experiences." *World Economy 13:* 1–14.

Edwards, S., and Edwards, A. C. 1991. *Monetarism and Liberalization: the Chilean Experiment.* Cambridge, Mass.: Ballinger Publishing.

Ehrlich, Isaac. 1990. "The Problem of Development: Introduction." *Journal of Political Economy 98:* S1–S11.

Elster, Jon. 1992. "On Doing What One Can." *East European Constitutional Review 1:* 15–17.

Elster, Jon, and Rune Slagstad, eds. 1988. *Constitutionalism and Democracy.* Cambridge: Cambridge University Press.

Evans, Peter B. 1989. "Predatory, Developmental, and Other Apparatuses: A Comparative Political Economy Perspective on the Third World State." *Sociological Forum 4:* 561–587.

Evans, Peter. 1992. "The State as a Problem and Solution: Predation, Embedded Autonomy, and Structural Change." In S. Haggard and R. Kaufman, eds., *The Politics of Economic Adjustment* (pp. 139–181) Princeton, N.J.: Princeton University Press.

Faini, Riccardo, Jaime de Melo, Abdel Senhadji-Semlali, and Julie Stanton. 1989. "Macro Performance under Adjustment Lending." World Bank. Country Economics Department. WPS 190. Washington, D.C.

Fanelli, J., Frenkel, R., and Rozenwurcel, G. 1990. "Growth and Structural Reform in Latin America: Where We Stand." Report prepared for UNCTAD. Buenos Aires: CEDES, October.

Feldman, Arnold J., Jorge R. Menés, and Natalia García Pardo. 1989. "La estructura social y el apoyo partidista en España." *Revista Española de Investigaciónes Sociologicas 47:* 7–72.

Fernandez, Raquel, and Dani Rodrik. 1991. "Resistance to Reforms: Status Quo Bias in the Presence of Individually Specific Uncertainty." *American Economic Review 81:* 1146–1155.

Fields, Gary S. 1988. "Income Distribution and Economic Growth." In Gustav Ranis and T. Paul Schults, eds., *The State of Development Economics* (pp. 459–485). Oxford: Basil Blackwell.

Findlay, Ronald. 1990. "The New Political Economy: Its Explanatory Power for the LDCs." *Economics and Politics 2:* 193–221.

Fischer, Stanley. 1991. Comment in the panel discussion. In M. Bruno, S. Fischer, E. Helpman, N. Liviatan, and L. Meridor, eds., *Lessons of Economic Stabilization and Its Aftermath* (pp. 276–280). Cambridge, Mass.: MIT Press.

Fishman, Robert M. 1990. "Rethinking State and Regime: Southern Europe's Transition to Democracy." *World Politics 42:* 422–440.

Frenkel, Jacob. 1991. Comment in the panel discussion. In M. Bruno, S. Fischer, E. Helpman, N. Liviatan, and L. Meridor, eds., *Lessons of Economic Stabilization and Its Aftermath* (pp. 400–404). Cambridge, Mass.: MIT Press.

Gourevitch, Peter. 1979. "The Reemergence of 'Peripheral Nationalisms': Some Comparative Speculations on the Spatial Distribution of Political Leadership and Economic Growth." *Comparative Studies in Society and History 21:* 303–322.

Grassi, Davide. 1991. "Economic and Organizational Determinants of Wage Restraint in New Democracies." Unpublished manuscript. University of Chicago.

Grilli, Vittorio, Donato Masciandaro, and Guido Tabellini. 1991. "Political and Monetary Institutions and Public Financial Policies in the Industrial Countries." *Economic Policy 13:* 341–392.

Grosfeld, Irena. 1991. "Privatization of State Enterprises in Eastern Europe." *Eastern European Politics and Societies 5:* 142–173.

Grossman, Gene M. 1990. "Promoting New Industrial Activities: A Survey of Recent Arguments and Evidence." *OECD Economic Studies,* No. 14, Spring.

Gunther, Reinhard, Giacomo Sani, and Goldie Shabad. 1986. *Spain after Franco: The Making of a Competitive Party System.* Berkeley: University of California Press.

Habermas, Jürgen. 1975. *Legitimation Crisis.* Boston: Beacon.

Haggard, Stephan. 1990. *Pathways from the Periphery: The Politics of Growth in the Newly Industrializing Countries.* Ithaca, N.Y.: Cornell Unversity Press.

Haggard, Stephan, and Robert R. Kaufman, eds. 1992. *The Politics of Economic Adjustment: International Constraints, Distributive Politics and the State.* Princeton, N.J.: Princeton University Press.

Haggard, Stephan, Robert Kaufman, Karim Shariff, and Steven B. Webb. 1990. "Politics, Inflation and Stabilization in Middle-Income Countries." Manuscript, World Bank, Washington, D.C.

Hardin, Russell. 1987. Why a Constitution?." Unpublished manuscript, University of Chicago.

Horowitz, Donald. 1991. *A Democratic South Africa.* Berkeley: University of California Press.

IMF (International Monetary Fund). 1992. *World Economic Outlook.* May. Washington, D.C.: IMF.

IMF (International Monetary Fund). 1993. *World Economic Outlook.* May. Washington, D.C.: IMF.

Jackman, Robert W. 1987. "Political Institutions and Voter Turnout in Industrial Democracies." *American Political Science Review 81:* 405–423.

King, Gary. 1989. "Representation through Legislative Redistricting: A Stochastic Model." *American Journal of Political Science 33:* 787–824.

King, Gary. 1990. "Electoral Representativeness and Partisan Bias in Multiparty Democracies." *Legislative Studies Quarterly 15:* 159–181.

King, Gary, and Robert X. Browning. 1987. "Democratic Representation and Partisan Bias in Congress." *American Political Science Review 81:* 1251–1276.

King, Gary, et al. 1990. "A Unified Model of Cabinet Dissolution in Parliamentary Democracies." *American Journal of Political Science 34:* 846–871.

Knight, Jack. 1992. *Institutions and Social Conflict.* Cambridge University Press.

Kolarska-Bobińska, Lena. 1989. "Poczucie niesprawiedliwości, konfliktu i preferowany ład w gospodarce." In *Polacy 88.* Warsaw: CPBP.

Kolarska-Bobińska, Lena. 1991. "Preferowany ład gospodarczy i opcje polityczno-ekonomiczne: poczatek okresu transformacji." In *Polacy 90.* Warsaw: CPBP.

Kornai, Janos. 1986. "The Soft Budget Constraint." *Kyklos 39:* 3– 30.

Kornai, Janos. 1990. *The Road to a Free Economy.* New York: Norton.

Krueger, Anne. 1991. *Economic Policy Reforms in Developing Countries.* Oxford: Blackwell.

Kurczewska, J., K. Staszyńska, and H. Bojar. 1993. "Blokady społeczeństwa obywatelskiego: słabe społeczeństwo obywatelskie i słabe państwo." In Andrzej Rychard and Michał Fedorowicz, eds., *Społeczeństwo w Transformacji* (pp. 84–96). Warsaw: IFiS PAN.

Laitin, David. 1987. "South Africa: Violence, Myths, and Democratic Reform." *World Politics 39*: 258–279.

Laitin, David. 1989. "Linguistic Revival: Politics and Culture in Catalonia." *Comparative Studies in Society and History 31:* 297–317.

Lamounier, Bolivar, ed. 1992. *Ouvindo o Brasil: Uma análise da opiniao pública Brasileira hoje.* São Paulo: Editora Sumaré.

Lane, Frederic C. 1979. *Profits from Power: Readings in Protection Rent and Violence Controlling Enterprises.* Albany: State University of New York Press.

Lechner, Norbert. 1985. "Pacto social nos procesos de democratizacao: a experiencia Latino-Americana." *Novos Estudos 13:* 29–44.

Lee, Jeong-Hwa, and Adam Przeworski. 1993. "Cui Bono? Social Democracy and Welfare." Unpublished manuscript, University of Chicago.

Levine, Ross, and David Renelt. 1991. "A Sensitivity Analysis of Cross-country Growth Regressions." World Bank Working Paper WPS 609, Washington, D.C.

Lieberson, Stanley, with Lynn Hansen. 1974. "National Development, Mother-Tongue Diversity, and the Comparative Study of Nations." *American Sociological Review 39:* 523–41.

Lijphart, Arend. 1977. *Democracy in Plural Societies.* New Haven, Conn.: Yale University Press.

Lijphart, Arend. 1984. *Democracies: Patterns of Majoritarian and Consensus Government in Twenty-one Countries.* New Haven, Conn.: Yale University Press.

Lijphart, Arend. 1989. "Democratic Political Systems: Types, Cases, Causes, and Consequences." *Journal of Theoretical Politics 1*: 33–48.

Lijphart, Arend. 1990. "The Political Consequences of Electoral Laws 1945–1985." *American Political Science Review 83*: 481–496.

Lijphart, Arend. 1991. "Constitutional Choices for New Democracies." *Journal of Democracy 2*: 72–84.

Linz, Juan J. 1994. "Presidential or Parliamentary Democracy: Does It Make a Difference?" In Juan J. Linz and Arturo Valenzuela, eds., *The Failure of Presidential Democracy.* Baltimore: The Johns Hopkins University Press.

Linz, Juan J., and Alfred Stepan. 1992. "Political Identities and Electoral Sequences: Spain, the Soviet Union and Yugoslavia." *Daedalus 121:* 123–39.

Lipset, Seymour M. 1960. *Political Man.* Garden City, N.Y.: Doubleday.

Lipton, David, and Jeffrey Sachs. 1990. "Creating a Market Economy in Eastern Europe: The Case of Poland." *Brookings Papers on Economic Activity 1:* 75–148.

Lopez, Juan J. 1991. "Political Determinants of Private Investment in Argentina: Field Work Impressions." Unpublished manuscript, University of Chicago.

Lucas, Robert E., Jr. 1988. "On the Mechanics of Economic Development." *Journal of Monetary Economics 22:* 3–42.

Lustick, Ian. 1979. "Stability in Deeply Divided Societies: Consociationalism or Control." *World Politics 31:* 325–344.

Maddison, Angus. 1982. *Phases of Capitalist Development.* Oxford University Press.

Mainwaring, Scott. 1992. "Presidentialism, Multipartism, and Democracy: The Difficult Combination." *Comparative Political Studies 26:* 198–228.

Manin, Bernard. 1995. "Les principes du gouvernement répresentatif." In *La démocratie des Modernes.* Paris: Arman Colin.

Maravall, José María. 1981. *La politica de la transición, 1975–1980.* Madrid: Taurus.

Maravall, José María. 1993. "Politics and Policy: Economic Reforms in Southern Europe." In Luiz Carlos Bresser Pereira, José María Maravall, and Adam Przeworski, *Economic Reforms in New Democracies: A Social-Democratic Approach* (pp. 77–131). Cambridge: Cambridge University Press.

Marer, Paul. 1991. "The Transition to a Market Economy in Eastern Europe." *OECD Observer,* No. 169 (April–May).

Marsh, Robert M. 1988. "Sociological Explanations of Economic Growth." *Studies in Comparative International Research 13:* 41–76.

Marshall, T. H. 1964. *Class, Citizenship and Social Development.* New York: Doubleday.

Masciandrano, Donato, and Guido Tabellini. 1988. "Monetary Regimes and Fiscal Deficits: A Comparative Analysis." In H. S. Cheng, ed., *Monetary Policy in Pacific Basin Countries* (pp.125–152). Dordrecht: Kluwer Academic.

McKinnon, Ronald I. 1991. *The Order of Economic Liberalization: Financial Control in the Transition to a Market Economy.* Baltimore: The Johns Hopkins University Press.

Meyer, John W., Michael T. Hannan, Richard Rubinson, and George M. Thomas. 1979. "National Economic Development, 1950–70: Social and Political Factors." In John W. Meyer and Michael Hannan, eds., *National Development and the World System: Educational, Economic and Political Change, 1950–1970* (pp. 85–116). Chicago: University of Chicago Press.

Miliband, Ralph. 1975. *Parliamentary Socialism: A Study in the Politics of Labour.* London: Merlin, 2nd edition.

Mill, John Stuart. 1958. *Considerations on Representative Government.* New York: Liberal Arts Press.

Minsky, Harold. 1986. *Stabilizing an Unstable Economy.* New Haven, Conn.: Yale University Press.

Moene, Karl Ove, and Michael Wallerstein. 1992. "The Decline of Social Democracy." Paper presented at the Annual Meeting of the American Political Science Association, Chicago, August.

Moisés, José Alvaro. 1990. "Eleições, Paricipação e Cultura Política: Mudanças e Continuidades." *Lua Nova 22:* 27–41.

Montero, José Ramón, and Mariano Torcal. 1990. "La cultura política de los Españoles: pautas de continuidad y cambio." *Sistema 90:* 39–74.

Morales, Juan Antonio. 1991. "The Transition from Stabilization to Sustained Growth in Bolivia." In Bruno, Fischer, Helpman, Liviatan, and Meridor, eds., *Lessons of*

Economic Stabilization and Its Aftermath (pp. 15–47). Cambridge, Mass.: MIT Press.

Moreno Ocampo, Luis. 1991. "Justicia y derechos humanos: Balance y futuro." Paper presented at the seminar "Derechos Humanos, Justicia, Política y Sociedad." September 20–21, Centro de Estudios de Estado y Sociedad, CEDS, Buenos Aires.

Mueller, Dennis. C. 1991. "Choosing a Constitution in East Europe: Lessons from Public Choice." *Journal of Comparative Economics 15*: 325–348.

Muller, Edward. 1988. "Democracy, Economic Development, and Income Inequality." *American Sociological Review 53:* 50–68.

Murrell, Peter. 1991. "Can Neoclassical Economics Underpin the Reform of Centrally Planned Economies?" *Journal of Economic Perspectives 5*: 59–76.

Nelson, Joan. 1984. "The Politics of Stabilization." In R. E. Feinberg and V. Kallab, eds., *Adjustment Crisis in the Third World.* New Brunswick, N.J.: Transaction.

Nelson, Joan, ed. 1990. *Economic Crisis and Policy Choice.* Princeton, N.J.: Princeton University Press.

O'Donnell, Guillermo. 1991. "Argentina, de nuevo." Working Paper No. 152. Hellen Kellogg Institute for International Studies, Notre Dame, Ind.

O'Donnel, Guillermo. 1992. "Delegative Democracy?" East–South Systems Transformation, University of Chicago, Working Paper No. 21.

O'Donnell, Guillermo, and Philippe C. Schmitter. 1986. *Transitions from Authoritarian Rule: Tentative Conclusions about Uncertain Democracies.* Baltimore: Johns Hopkins University Press.

OECD (Organisation for Economic Cooperation and Development). 1990. "Transition from the Command to Market Economy." Manuscript summary of a meeting held at the Vienna Institute for Comparative Economic Studies. Paris: OECD.

Olson, Mancur, Jr. 1991. "Autocracy, Democracy and Prosperity." In Richard J. Zeckhauser, ed., *Strategy and Choice* (pp. 131–157). Cambridge, Mass.: MIT Press.

Ortuño-Ortin, Ignacio, John Roemer, and Joaquim Silvestre. 1993. "Investment Planning in Market Socialism." In Samuel Bowles, Herbert Gintis, and Bo Gustafsson, eds., *Markets and Democracy: Participation, Accountability and Efficiency* (pp. 279–305). Cambridge: Cambridge University Press.

Ozbudun, Ergun. 1992. "Constitution-Making in Democratic Transitions." East–South Systems Transformations, University of Chicago, Working Paper No. 20.

Parkin, Michael. 1986. "Domestic Monetary Institutions and Deficits." In J. M. Buchanan, C. K. Rowley, and R. D. Tollison, eds., *Deficits.* New York: Basil Blackwell.

Persson, Torsten, and Guido Tabellini. 1991. "Is Inequality Harmful for Growth? Theory and Evidence." Working Paper No. 91-155. Department of Economics, University of California, Berkeley.

Powell, G. B., Jr. 1981. "Party Systems and Political System Performance in Contemporary Democracies." *American Political Science Review 75:* 861–879.

Powell, G. B., Jr. 1982. *Contemporary Democracies: Participation, Stability and Violence.* Cambridge, Mass.: Harvard University Press.

Powell, G. B., Jr. 1986. "American Voters Turnout in Comparative Perspective." *American Political Science Review 80:* 17–44.

Powell, G. B., Jr. 1989. "Constitutional Design and Citizen Electoral Control." *Journal of Theoretical Politics 1:* 107–130.

Powell, G. B., Jr. 1990. "Holding Governments Accountable: How Constitutional Arrangements and Party Systems Affect Clarity of Responsibility for Policy in Contemporary Democracies." Unpublished manuscript, University of Rochester.

Powell, G. B., Jr. 1992. "Liberal Democracies." In Mary Hawkesworth and Maurice Kogan, eds., *Encyclopaedia of Government and Politics.* New York: Routledge.

Poznański, Kazimierz. 1991. "Poland's Transition to Capitalism." Unpublished manuscript, Warsaw, SGIPS.

Przeworski, Adam. 1990. *The State and the Economy under Capitalism. Fundamentals of Pure and Applied Economics, Vol. 40.* Chur: Harwood Academic.

Przeworski, Adam. 1991. *Democracy and the Market: Political and Economic Reforms in Eastern Europe and Latin America.* Cambridge University Press.

Przeworski, Adam. 1993a. "Economic Reforms, Public Opinion, and Political Institutions: Poland in the Eastern European Perspective." In Luiz Carlos Bresser Pereira, José María Maravall, and Adam Przeworski. *Economic Reforms in New Democracies: A Social-Democratic Approach* (pp. 132–198). Cambridge University Press.

Przeworski, Adam. 1993b. "Intertemporal Politics: Public Support for Economic Reforms in Poland." Paper presented at the Conference on Political Dynamics of Economic Reforms, University of Chicago, May 14–16.

Przeworski, Adam. 1993c. "Socialism and Social Democracy." In Joel Krieger, ed. *The Oxford Companion to Politics of the World* (pp. 832–839). Oxford: Oxford University Press.

Przeworski, Adam, and Fernando Limongi. 1993. "Modernization: Theory and Facts." Working Paper No. 4. Chicago Center on Democracy, University of Chicago.

Przeworski, Adam, and Michael Wallerstein. 1982. "The Structure of Class Conflict in Democratic Capitalist Societies." *American Political Science Review 76:* 215–236.

Rabushka, Alvin, and Kenneth Shepsle. 1972. *Politics in Plural Societies: A Theory of Democratic Instability.* Columbus, Ohio: Merrill.

Rae, D. W. 1967. *The Political Consequences of Electoral Laws.* New Haven, Conn.: Yale University Press.

Rainwater, Lee, Barbara Torrey, and Timothy Smeeding. 1989. "Poverty and Low Incomes: International Evidence from Household Income Surveys." Unpublished manuscript, Paris, OECD.

Remmer, Karen L. 1986. "The Politics of Economic Stabilization: IMF Standby Programs in Latin America, 1954–1984." *Comparative Politics 19:* 1–24.

Remmer, Karen L. 1990. "Democracy and Economic Crisis: The Latin American Experience." *World Politics 42:* 315–325.

Rhee, Sungsup. 1987. "Policy Reforms of the Eighties and Industrial Adjustments in Korean Economy." KDI Working Paper No. 8708. Seoul: Korea Development Institute.

Robinson, Donald L. 1991. "The Comparative Study of Constitutions: Suggestions for Organizing the Inquiry." *Political Science and Politics 24:* 272–280.

Rodrik, Dani. 1991. "Policy Uncertainty and Private Investment in Developing Countries." *Journal of Development Economics 36:* 229–242.

Rodrik, Dani. 1992. "Making Sense of the Soviet Trade Shock in Eastern Europe: A Framework and Some Estimates." Unpublished manuscript. Columbia University.

Roemer, John. 1991. "Would Economic Democracy Decrease the Amount of Public Bads?" University of California at Davis, Department of Economics, Working Paper No. 376.

Romer, Paul M. 1990. "Endogenous Technical Change." *Journal of Political Economy 98:* S71–S103.

Rosati, Dariusz. 1993. "Poland: Glass Half Empty." In Richard Portes, ed., *Economic Transformation in Eastern Europe: A Progress Report* (pp. 211–273). London: Centre for Economic Policy Research.

Rueschemeyer, Dietrich, Evelyne Huber Stephens, and John D. Stephens. 1992. *Capitalist Development and Democracy.* Chicago: University of Chicago Press.

Rychard, Andrzej. 1991. "Politics and Society after the Breakthrough: the Source and Threats to Political Legitimacy in Post-communist Poland." In G. Sanford, ed., *Democratization in Poland.* London: Macmillan.

Sabino, Fernando. 1991. *Zélia, uma paixão.* Rio de Janeiro: Editora Record.

Sadowski, Zdzisław, Maciej Iwanek, and Jozef Najdek. 1990. "An Overview of the Process of Change in Poland." Paper presented at Conference on East European Reform Towards Market Economy and the OECD, Vienna, 14–16 March.

Sah, Raj, and Martin Weitzman. 1991. "A Proposal for Using Incentive Precommitments in Public Enterprise Funding." *World Development 19:* 595–605.

Saunders, Peter, and Friedrich Klau. 1985. *The Role of the Public Sector: Causes and Consequences. OECD Economic Studies, No. 4.* Paris: OECD.

Schelling, Thomas. 1963. *The Strategy of Conflict.* Cambridge, Mass.: Harvard University Press.

Schelling, Thomas. 1978. *Micromotives and Macrobehavior.* New York: Norton.

Schmitter, Philippe C. 1984. "Patti e transizioni: mezzi non-democratici a fini democratici," *Rivista Italiana di Scienza Politica 14:* 363–382.

Schmitter, Philippe C. 1991. "The International Context for Contemporary Democratization: Constraints and Opportunities upon the Choice of National Institutions and Policies." East–South Systems Transformations, University of Chicago, Working Paper No. 8.

Shugart, Matthew Soberg, and John M. Carey. 1992. *Presidents and Assemblies: Constitutional Design and Electoral Dynamics.* Cambridge University Press.

Solimano, Andres. 1992. "After Socialism and Dirigisme: Which Way?" World Bank. Policy Research Working Papers. WPS 981. Washington, D.C.

Stallings, Barbara. 1992a. "International Influence in Economic Policy: Debt, Stabilization, and Structural Reform." In Stephan Haggard and Robert Kaufman, eds., *The Politics of Economic Adjustment: International Constraints, Distributive Politics and the State* (pp. 41–88). Princeton, N.J.: Princeton University Press.

Stallings, Barbara. 1992b. "The New International Context of Development." Global Studies Research Program, University of Wisconsin, Working Paper No. 1.

Stallings, Barbara, and Robert Kaufuman, eds. 1989. *Debt and Democracy in Latin America.* Boulder: Westview Press.

Staniszkis, Jadwiga. 1992. "Main Paradoxes of the Democratic Chance in Eastern Europe." In Kazimierz Z. Poznanski, ed., *Constructing Capitalism: The Reemergence of Civil Society and Liberal Economy in the Post-Communist World.* Boulder: Westview Press.

Stepan, Alfred. 1978. *The State and Society: Peru in Comparative Perspective.* Princeton, N.J.: Princeton University Press.

Stepan, Alfred, and Cindy Skach. 1992. "Meta-institutional Frameworks and Democratic Consolidation." East–South Systems Transformations, University of Chicago, Working Paper No. 21.

Stigler, George. 1975. *The Citizen and the State: Essays on Regulation.* Chicago: University of Chicago Press.

Stiglitz, Joseph A. 1991. "Wither Socialism? Perspectives from the Economics of Information." Wicksel Memorial Lecture. Unpublished manuscript.

Stiglitz, Joseph. 1992. "The Design of Financial Systems for the Newly Emerging Democracies of Eastern Europe." In Christopher Clague and Gordon Rausser, eds., *The Emergence of Market Economies in Eastern Europe* (pp. 161–184). Oxford: Blackwell.

Stokes, Susan Carol. 1993. "Economic Reforms and Public Opinion in Fujimori's Peru." Paper presented at the Conference on Political Dynamics of Economic Reforms, University of Chicago, May 14–16.

Strom, Kaare. 1985. "Party Goals and Government Performance in Parliamentary Democracies." *American Political Science Review 79:* 738–754.

Strom, Kaare. 1990. *Minority Government and Majority Rule.* Cambridge: Cambridge University Press.

Summers, Robert, Irving B. Kravis, and Alan Heston. 1984. "Changes in the World Income Distribution." *Journal of Policy Modeling 6:* 237–269.

Swank, Duane. 1992. "Politics and the Structural Dependence of the State in Democratic Capitalist Nations." *American Political Science Review 86:* 38–54.

Tanzi, Vito. 1989. "Fiscal Policy, Stabilization and Growth." In Mario I. Blejer and Ke-young Chu, eds., *Fiscal Policy, Stabilization, and Growth in Developing Countries* (pp. 13–32). Washington, D.C.: IMF.

Tarkowski, Jacek. 1989. "Old and New Patterns of Corruption in Poland and the USSR." *Telos 80:* 51–63.

Tollison, Robert D. 1982. "Rent Seeking: A Survey." *Kyklos 35:* 575–602.

UNICEF. 1994. "Crisis in Mortality, Health and Nutrition." *Economies in Transition Studies. Regional Monitoring Report No. 2.* Florence, Italy: UNICEF.

Vickers, J., and G. Yarrow. 1991. "Economic Perspectives on Privatization." *Journal of Economic Perspectives 5:* 111–132.

von Thadden, E. L. 1991. "Bank Finance and Long-term Investment." WWZ Discussion Paper, University of Basel.

Wade, Robert. 1990. *Governing the Market: Economic Theory and the Role of Government in East Asian Industrialization.* Princeton, N.J.: Princeton University Press.

Weaver, R. Kent, and Bert A. Rockman. 1993. "Institutional Reform and Constitutional Design." In R. Kent Weaver and Bert A. Rockman, eds., *Do Institutions Matter?* (pp. 462–482). Washington, D.C.: Brookings Institution.

Weffort, Francisco. 1991. "New Democracies, Which Democracies?" East–South Systems Transformations, University of Chicago, Working Paper No. 15.

Westphal, Larry E. 1990. "Industrial Policy in an Export-Propelled Economy: Lessons from South Korea's Experience." *Journal of Economic Perspectives 4*: 1395–1424.

Whitehead, Laurence. 1991. "The International Dimension of Democratization: A Survey of the Alternatives." Paper presented at the Fifteenth Congress of the IPSA, Buenos Aires.

Williamson, John. 1990. "What Washington Means by Policy Reform." In John Williamson, ed., *Latin American Adjustment: How Much Has Happened?* (pp. 5–20). Washington, D.C.: Institute of International Economics.

World Bank. 1987. *World Development Report, 1987.* Washington, D.C.: World Bank.

World Bank. 1991. *World Development Report, 1991.* Washington, D.C.: World Bank.

World Bank. 1992. *World Development Report, 1992.* Washington, D.C.: World Bank.

Zimmerman, Ekkart. 1987. "Government Stability in Six European Countries during the World Economic Crisis of the 1930s: Some Preliminary Considerations." *European Journal of Political Research 15:* 23–52.

Zimmerman, Ekkart. 1988. "Economic and Political Reactions to the World Economic Crisis of the 1930s in Six European Countries." *International Studies Quarterly 32:* 305–334.

East–South Systems Transformations
Working Papers

19. Adam Przeworski, "Economic Reforms in New Democracies: Poland in the Eastern European Perspective" (November 1991).
20. Ergun Ozbudun, "Constitution Making in Democratic Transitions" (December 1991).
21. Guillermo O'Donnell, "Delegative Democracy?" (December 1991).

About the Authors

PRANAB BARDHAN is Professor of Economics at the University of California, Berkeley, and chief editor of the *Journal of Development Economics*.

LUIZ CARLOS BRESSER PEREIRA is currently Brazil's Minister of Administrative Reform and served as Minister of Finance in 1987–88. He is Professor of Economics at the Fundação Getúlio Vargas in São Paulo and the editor of the *Revista de Economia Política*.

LÁSZLÓ BRUSZT is Professor of Political Science at the Central European University in Budapest.

JANG JIP CHOI is Professor of Political Science at Korea University in Seoul, South Korea.

ELLEN TURKISH COMISSO is Professor of Political Science at the University of California, San Diego.

ZHIYUAN CUI is Assistant Professor of Political Science at the Massachusetts Institute of Technology.

TORCUATO DI TELLA is Professor of Sociology at the University of Buenos Aires and coordinator of the Center for Latin American Studies at the Instituto del Servicio Exterior de la Nación in Buenos Aires. He is also a founder and member of the Board of the Instituto Di Tella.

ELEMER HANKISS is Professor of Political Science at the University of Budapest and Research Director at the Institute of Sociology of the Hungarian Academy of Sciences. He is the former Head of National Television, Hungary.

LENA KOLARSKA-BOBIŃSKA is the Director of the Center for Research on Public Opinion, Warsaw, Poland.

DAVID LAITIN is the William R. Kenan, Jr., Professor of Political Science and Director of the Center for the Study of Politics, History and Culture (Wilder House) at the University of Chicago.

JOSÉ MARÍA MARAVALL is Professor of Sociology at the Instituto Juan March de Investigaciones Sociales and the Universidad Complutense, Madrid, Spain. He has served as Spain's Minister of Education.

ANDRANIK MIGRANYAN is a Research Fellow at the Institute of Economic Science of the Russian Academy of Sciences, Moscow, Russia.

GUILLERMO O'DONNELL is the Hellen Kellogg Professor of Government and International Studies and Academic Director of the Kellogg Institute for International Studies, Notre Dame University. He is former President of the International Political Science Association.

ERGUN OZBUDUN is Professor of Sociology at University of Ankara, Turkey, and the President of the Turkish Foundation for Democracy.

ADAM PRZEWORSKI is the Martin A. Ryerson Distinguished Service Professor of Political Science and the Director of the Chicago Center on Democracy at the University of Chicago.

JOHN E. ROEMER is the Professor of Economics and Director of the Program on Economy, Justice and Society at the University of California, Davis.

PHILIPPE C. SCHMITTER is Professor of Political Science at Stanford University.

BARBARA STALLINGS is Director of the Economic Development Division of the United Nations Economic Commission for Latin American and the Caribbean, Santiago, Chile. She is also Chair of the Joint Committee on Latin American Studies of the SSRC and ACLS.

ALFRED STEPAN is the Rector of the Central European University in Budapest.

FRANCISCO WEFFORT is Brazil's Minister of Culture and Professor of Political Science at the University of São Paulo.

JERZY J. WIATR is Professor of Sociology at the University of Warsaw and a Deputy to the Polish Parliament.

Author Index

Subject Index